Tikkunim (Corrections)

by

Jesse Bogner

For the people who want to
disarm the world crisis with
new values.

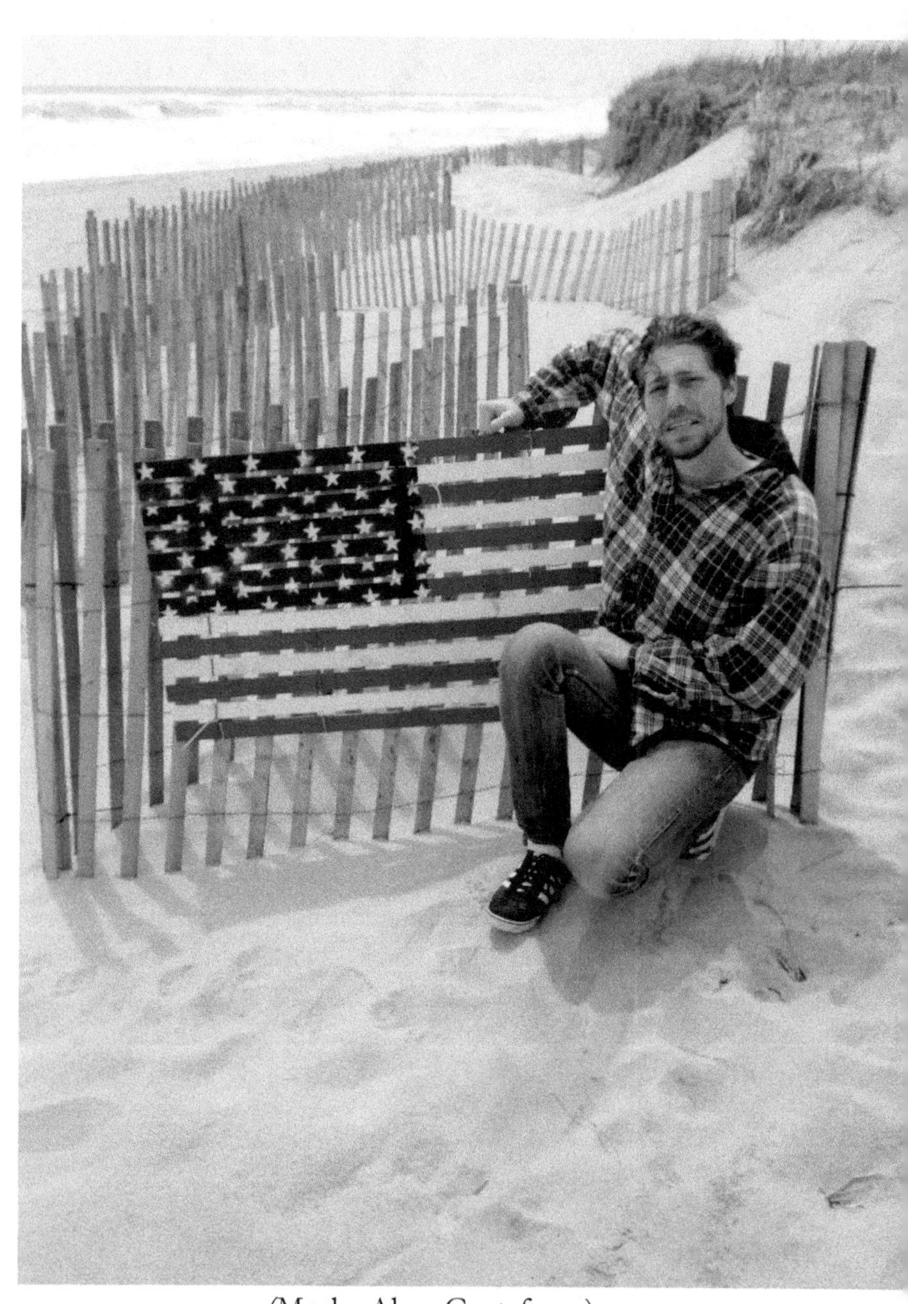

(Me, by Alma Gustafsson)

Contents

Introduction

INTRODUCTION

After the publication of my first book, *The Egotist*, I began writing articles about politics and the spiritual roots of a world in crisis. A world of contradictions that reveals the flawed development of man using rational systems. These rational systems that cannot cope with an irrational world and the seemingly irrational nature of the creatures that inhabit it. It began as supplemental work to the novel I was working on, before becoming an obsession, a calling from above.

Like everyone else, I was caught up in the oddest election cycle in American history. Unlike just about everyone else, I predicted Trump's victory four months before he was elected, without flinching when the New York Times only gave him an 8% chance on election night. I felt the vitriol of a nation torn apart that was tired of being lied to, passed over and forgotten by a small elite minority. I locked into this tenor of American life living 7000 miles away in Israel, reading everything I could get my hands on.

The more I explored political tropes, the more my perception changed. Beginning my writings as one of the last vehemently pro-Israel leftists, it slowly became apparent to me that the Democratic Party like most of the left of center parties in Europe had degraded itself to the point that it had reversed nearly every position JFK and Martin Luther King would have fought for. It was clear that beneath the surface both parties were not at all what they purported to be, but the Democrats were the real wolves in sheep's clothing.

I proclaimed myself a Republican after a lot of resistance to the political positions of my conservative-leaning spiritual teacher. His spiritual understanding of the world gave him opposite perception of reality that he sensed almost unconsciously, which I could only find to be the case through heavy embittered research. After Trump's election, everything became clear. Nothing was as it seemed.

I used my highly rational mind as a tool to illustrate how the world was no longer rational. Though politics was the specter to look at the world's contradictory and destructive developments, I felt the source of all these troubles came from a spiritual source, a fundamental lack of connection between people.

The earth is crying out for its correction and Kabbalah is its remedy. Kabbalah is the method to reveal "the world to come" in one's lifetime. A tool that connects the corporeal world to the spiritual plane that contains a memory of and all the force of all the great spiritual titans of Israel. From the last great late Kabbalist, the Rabash to his father Baal HaSulam, to the Baal Shem Tov, to Moses and Abraham, all these souls leave an imprint that exists for eternity and anyone with a desire can access them by entering the spiritual realms above our world. Spiritual realms that direct everything under the rule of one ultimate authority known as the Creator.

I want you all to enter a world of endless love that orients all of corporeality and gives each person on this earth exactly what he or she needs to live in permanence and perfection, if one firmly chooses salvation above all else. My great hope is that by understanding our shattered world, you will be inspired to realize the means of correcting it.

As the great Rabash writes, "We were given the path of faith, which is above reason, namely not to take our sensations and reason into account, but say, as it is written, "They have eyes and see not. They have ears and hear not." Rather, we should believe that the Creator is certainly the Messiah, and He knows what is good for me and what is not good for me. Therefore, He wants me to feel my state as I do, and for myself, I do not care how I feel myself because I want to work in order to bestow.

"Therefore, the main thing is that I need to work for the Creator. And although I feel that there is no wholeness in my work, still, in the Kelim (vessels) of the upper one, meaning from the perspective of the upper one, I am utterly complete, as it is written, "The cast out will not be cast out from Him." Hence, I am satisfied with my work—that I have the privilege of serving the King even at the lowest degree. That, too, I regard as a great privilege that the Creator has allowed me come closer to Him."

How the New New Left Turned Me into a Conservative Against My Will

PART ONE: THE WRITINGS ON THE WALL

(Me and my brother Miles, by Dawn Neway)

As a precocious child of eight and then nine who idolized Kurt Cobain and Thomas Jefferson, I was a conservative living in Connecticut, because my parents were conservatives. Bill Clinton's reelection campaign changed that for me and many others. While my mother stuck to her guns, my father and most sensible non-religious people of the Rockefeller Republican school supported Clinton, because his policies were mostly conservative and he wasn't infected with the backwards ideals of evangelical Christianity that neocons saturated into American culture.

(My Mom, by Miles Bogner)

It didn't hurt that it felt like the market was giving away free money. The 96 election against the likable Bob Dole was an embarrassment to the Republican party. The Democrats looked like an unstoppable force. This is why the Republicans did everything in their power to discredit Bill.

When George W. Bush bankrupted the country with insane spending, wars against the wrong enemies and poorly thought out tax cuts for the rich, the errors of the Republican party were all too clear. Coupled with that, I was very influenced by the media, especially the Fahrenheit 9/11 propaganda and countless other documentaries that showed the immoral corporate structure for what it was, that took pleasure in representing Republicans as incompetent morons taking bribes from oil dictatorships and lobbyists. I was almost unaware of the hypocrisy of the Democrats doing the same thing. Driven by some combination of neoconservatism and Kissinger style globalism, the party I supported was also bought and sold for, obsessed with "morality" (2 Live Crew, heavy metal and violence in videogames), playing chess games and losing them in global warfare.

I read newspapers periodically, but in all honesty, I was much more interested in literature, film, music and drugs. I knew I couldn't change the world in any marked way, so I followed the news when I was in the mood (especially during election cycles) and developed as an individual, a huge egoist who was very proud of the thousands of hours I spent developing my mind through the films of ultra-leftist filmmakers like Jean Luc Godard.

When I was a liberal, it was OK to be entirely selfish. This political stance was an indicator of moral superiority to the homophobic, xenophobic masses that kept Bush in power for two terms.

I began to notice flaws in liberalism in my highly traditional boy school in New York City when I moved there a couple of weeks before 9/11. The Browning School, that graduated figures as diverse as Jamie Dimon, Henry Luce, too many Rockefellers to count and Howard Dean, was bastion of elite neoliberalism (about half our class was conservative, a real oddity in NYC), and still, half the faculty believed in the ideology of multiculturalism. It was the first time I became aware of flawed liberal ideals entering the chambers of what I assumed was the future elite.

There was an inability to look at history without judging the morals of early feminists (complete racists) and Thomas Jefferson (hypocrite lothario slaveowner) so much so that it would impede on our understanding of the actual events of American history, or how government worked. I saw the hypocrisy of this, the desire to group people and divide them in the service of inclusivity and feel a sense of catharsis by acknowledging how horrible the West is. The little work we did learning about lawmaking and the checks and balances of government were clearly relics of the past. Laws don't go through the same processes and parties no longer work together towards a greater good.

I also noticed that the faculty had become hypersensitive to the barely existent threat of racism, homophobia and sexism. The teachers casually invited us to protest Victoria's Secret on the Upper West Side for displays of beautiful airbrushed women and championed the un-American banning of smoking from bars.

As white boys of privilege, it was now our job to apologize for the maltreatment of everyone else throughout history. Never mind I was mostly Jewish and Eastern European, and thus my ancestors were the oppressed ones in most equations, I was not allowed to take pride in American values. They were the source of social injustice. I'm not lying, I was convinced I was a communist for a month or two, as a fifteen-year-old wearing Gucci loafers, whose main interests were related to the glorious decadence of David Bowie and punk rock. I thought all Republicans were evil racists. The idea had been force-fed. I would beg my Mom and Grandmothers to change parties, "Saddam Hussein had nothing to do with 9/11!!!"

When I got to Bard College in 2005, arguably the most liberal university in America, my agnosticism turned to atheism, but I knew myself better. Though I thought I was incapable of predicting my future failures, I found a new confidence and wanted to be great and wealthy, like 70s intellectuals who dated movie stars and drank scotch, pontificating as they slurred their words on talk shows.

In my mind, I was sort of living that lifestyle by proxy of my much richer friends. Two days into college, I was punished for skipping class, by an arrogant albeit talented novelist named Joydeep Roy-Bhattacharya, with an assignment to write a six-page apology letter saying how my time away from class was spent. It felt like 1984. Something sinister was happening there. I befriended the few people who had no interest in social Marxism, all the team-building and positivity orientation against bigotry, essentially all the precursors to safe spaces and trigger warnings I'm constantly hearing about on TV. Below is an excerpt from the apology.

Annabelle and Paris were in the room with a kid I vaguely knew of from New York named Theo. We talked for about twenty minutes. The conversation commenced on a very shallow level until we started finding our tastes were quite similar and began making each other laugh. Like Paris and Annabelle, we were turned off by the overtly utopian ideals of Bard. We wished we were better people, but found the concept of the Bard world impossible. As the day went on we realized this wasn't the case. It was OK that the people at Bard are too nice, too clever and essentially embrace their liberal leanings properly, before shutting down the opinions of others.

Writing this in 2005, I, and everyone else in the story is a liberal. Paris, my best friend, tragically died of a drug overdose that I partially blame on his disintegration into moral philosophy. Annabelle, I assume, is still a liberal with some conservative leanings. Theo is a smart liberal, a real prince, and one of my favorite people in the world. If he reads this, he and other people from my past might try and dissuade me from turning to the other side of the party aisle.

I was aware I was living in a bubble, an echo chamber of social Marxism. My agnosticism and curiosity with Buddhism and cultural Judaism were entirely forgotten. I still for the most part supported Israel, but reluctantly, as I again began seeing the victim vs. oppressor narrative everywhere. Watching a documentary on the 60s-counterculture terrorist organization The Weather Underground, we were implicitly being told to champion their rebellious stances, free love and innocence against an evil empire called the United States of America. Luckily, my generation was much more apolitical than the current one, because God knows what kind of reasonable people I would have found myself protesting.

With a few exceptions, college was very bad for me. Even my writing suffered at times from its exposure to literary theory, academic writing and classes like Race and Nature in Africa, which I only took because *Heart of Darkness* was on the reading list. I should have been aware they were going to try and ruin that book for me. I was an apolitical social liberal. I had heard musings that the media had become extremely partisan over the course of the

Bush administration, but I thought that was a positive step against a regime that was for Saudi Arabia and against rational thought, stem cell research and social egalitarianism.

The failure of the Bush administration swallowed most would-be conservatives from elite universities into liberals. Neoliberalism, the widespread policy of Thatcher and Reagan that was embraced by Clinton and Blair could not tolerate the Bush era spending and the greed of the big banks who depended on valueless mortgage-backed securities. Then the economy crumbled.

The 2008 financial crisis happened a year before my graduation. Publishing, the field I planned to enter (I wasn't thinking people would look at my GPA when I failed 4 classes, destroying what would have been perfectly acceptable) looked like one of the first casualties. In order to live in New York, you either had to enter finance, hustle drugs and real estate, or be supported by your parents. I was kind of of the latter category and expected everything would be handed to me, broke and drunk most of the time.

From time to time I would get writing gigs and take service-industry work, after my dream of working in publishing was killed by my entitled attitude and drug use, which got me fired from Details Magazine just as I was being given real stuff to do the day after my much older girlfriend broke up with me. Without alcohol, I was socially inept. I said very inappropriate things with it. I'm sure I made the people I worked with uncomfortable. With virtually no money and a designer wardrobe courtesy of my father, at night, I was partying with the New York elite at places like The Standard Hotel and The Beatrice Inn. Many of my friends, including famous rock stars and actors and many sons and daughters of celebrities and billionaires thought I was brilliant, but I had no tools to succeed in life. I was a blackout drunk without morality, who felt morally superior to Republicans.

(Me and Jonny Rooms hungover at WalMart, I think ironically, by Taline Arslanian)

I wanted a politician to save me. While I was later skeptical of nonsense like the occupy movement, I had faith in Obama. I wanted Hillary, but by the time he won the nomination, I loved the guy. He was a young brilliant black man with the same values I was indoctrinated with, who happened to have good taste for a Presidential candidate. The guy loved *The Wire* and read Joan Didion and Jonathan Franzen advance copies. I ignored his affiliation with Palestine, because I read PLO adviser Edward Said (who Obama had dinner with) on the first freaking day of school at Bard and he didn't seem as bad as my Dad made him out to be. It seemed clear Obama was going to get us out of wasteful, mismanaged wars in the Middle East, hold Wall Street accountable, bring jobs back and give us Universal healthcare.

Yes, ladies and gentlemen, social Marxism has had its turn in the White House for 8 years. As I've written about at length, Obama was not the savior of democracy the media paints him as. In spite of this, I blindly supported him, because he was on the surface much better than Bush. I avoided politics, drank and drugged a lot, got sober a few times, had jobs intermittently and did some very good writing that never got anywhere and was even paid to write an unpublished novel.

I was accidentally exposed to conservative values when I started listening to Adam Carolla make right-wing folksy, *A Face in the Crowd* style arguments from time to time, because I discovered podcasts early. He had guests like Andrew Breitbart, who the left basically equated to Hitler. While I mostly disagreed with him vehemently, I became aware of alternative thinking that was not as stupid, backwards or racist, as I had assumed all contemporary conservative thought was from listening to friends and Bill Maher monologues. The few conservative voices I respected, people like Peggy Noonan and George Will, were in my mind irrelevant relics, likely to shift party allegiance soon enough. Many of this small vocal minority of conservative intellectuals voted for Hillary on 2016.

When I began my studies in education (because I was unemployable), it was clear to me that the state exams tested ideological affiliation more than teaching proficiency. I saw how the left was slowly making conservative opinions unacceptable in society, actual becoming intolerant of some of the decidedly not racist teaching ideologies I preferred to multiculturalism that textbooks still acknowledged as valid. I began to get worried about the imminent dumbing down of the American electorate, that I was too blind to see had already happened.

When I moved to Israel to study and write books and articles on Kabbalah in 2013, American politics went on the back-burner. What could one man without a clear stance do? I became very concerned with Israel and the unjust way the media covered Israel. My blind acceptance of Israel and Obama were on a collision course. My stance became, I am the most liberal person in the world, except for the Israel issue.

In order to not be called a racist, what the BDS was branding as "apartheid" apology, I researched Muslim ideology, movements and governments. It was as fascinating as it was petrifying to someone living in a country bordered by Gaza, The West Bank, Libya, Syria and the slightly less insane nations of Egypt and Jordan. Though I was critical of US intervention in the Middle East in broad strokes, I didn't really blame Obama much, even though the only person Obama ever stood up to was Bibi Netanyahu.

Admittedly, I knew more about Brad Pitt and Angelina Jolie's kids than I did about the Arab Spring before this research began. When conservatives in Israel and abroad started to thrash my liberal articles making fun of Donald Trump and his obvious lying, I began researching the mostly fake accusations I was getting. I understood his appeal, unlike the mainstream media, who ripped apart the most effective convention speech I had ever seen.

I understood how much people hated Hillary. Watching the debates, I started to hate her and the anti-Semitic high school principal looking motherfucker who she chose as a running mate. This real fear she would lose, forced me to study the foreign policy of the Obama administration and investigate the emails that at first glance seemed like much ado but nothing. I thought I could convince people to vote for Hillary with facts in a post-fact world.

Two days before the election, a little wary of Hillary Clinton's connection to The Muslim Brotherhood and her collusion with the press, I wrote a long article about Trump's lying and how Facebook, supported by Breitbart, Russia (RT is operated by Russian government) and Assange reporting real and exaggerated faults with Clinton, created an environment wherein Trump could spread misinformation to an enthusiastic base of supporters who would get Trump elected.

After Brexit, I was all but convinced Trump would beat his poll numbers and a few days before the election, when I counted the electoral votes in Trump's favor courtesy of Nate Silver's FiveThirtyEight, he was winning in spite of being way behind in the popular vote. His odds were around 29%, but to me it was a certainty he would win. I wanted to wake up the left to this reality as best as I could and get them out to fight to prevent Trump's victory that represented the crumbling of the fourth estate as an institutional power. No one thought it was possible.

When I was watching the election coverage, I was shocked to see

Trump winning states that even I hadn't predicted. I noticed something change in me, as I watched the analysts, who by all accounts were supposed to be objective, in shock, clearly angered by the results. What I had heard Breitbart say in 2011 had finally sunken into my skull. Just like coverage of the Iran Deal, the liberal media had built an echo chamber that refused to acknowledge anything positive about Trump or negative about Hillary and it was sickening to me that she was aware of her allies funding Isis.

I was very confused. I didn't like Trump most of the time, but I did take pleasure in him skewering the faulty arguments of the left, who were apologizing for the hellholes that some American cities have become and the insistence that the economy was in good shape. And his unapologetic insistence of the clear reality that Putin has outsmarted her and Obama in Syria was refreshing. He could have easily added Crimea to the point if he had heard of the region. The day after the election, I wrote the following, still considering myself a liberal. I didn't really care he was lying, because Trump tells the truth even when he lies.

"I was tired of defending Obama and Clinton for accomplishing things like piss-poor healthcare reform and the inevitable step of marriage equality, when the world is shambles. I had a Howard Beale moment and got tired of the bullshit.

It just became so clear to me how backwards and broken our society is. How disconnected we are from each other. How we are lied to both in the obvious conspiracy theory, "Mexicans are rapists," "Killary Clinton" way and in the way that Obama and Hillary lie to us through omission and cozy relationships with reporters. I'm tired of clear acceptance that legal bribes are part of the political process. Say what you will about Donald Trump, when Prince Alwaleed, a Saudi billionaire and big Clinton Foundation contributor rightfully chastised Trump for calling on "a ban on all Muslims entering the country until we figure this thing out," Trump fought back beautifully in a tweet. "Dopey Prince @Alwaleed_Talal wants to control our U.S. politicians with daddy's money. Can't do it when I get elected.#Trump2016." Never mind that Trump started his business with "daddy's money." He stood up the evil powers that be, without an ounce of shame or apology, and yesterday Alwaleed congratulated Trump with his tail between his legs. Maybe this is what our country needs."

I was shocked no one was willing to give the crazy guy a chance, considering he was a Democrat a few years ago and advocated for a lot of the same things as Bernie Sanders, before asking for the help of both parties in his victory speech. My article was greeted with hate. I kept hearing things like, "How can you support a fascist?" "You know Hitler wasn't that concerned about the Jews at first?" "The first thing a Dictator does is discredit the media."

The adverse reaction of the vocal extremists of the left wing has been predictably absurd, but the response of moderate Democrats has been shocking. Not only are perfectly sane people wearing pussy-hats, but they're concocting wild conspiracy theories that a completely lost press reports on, usually as speculation, but sometimes not. The 17 government agencies agree on Russia's responsibility for the Clinton hack, though there is no evidence of this. The left is still being played by Putin. It's hard to blame liberals for believing these assertions, since they're presented as fact in The New Yorker and The New York Times. Putin wanted nothing more than getting credit for Trump's victory that proves to his people first and foremost that Russia is strong enough to intervene in US elections. It also doesn't hurt his argument that democracy is broken and no one is really free.

I can't really argue with him on that one, as partisanship has destroyed any free flow of ideas. Democrats discredit others, often with the race card. What people see as fascism from Trump has little relation to his policies, which are not really so different from deep state advocate, deporter in chief, Barack Obama, who I have said on many occasions funded Iran and armed Saudi Arabia to make sure the Sunnis and Shias keep funding ISIS style terrorism for the foreseeable future. When a party is no longer willing to listen to reason, or acknowledge fault, and is intolerant of opposition, I can no longer support them. I understand this is precisely what people say about Trump, but I'm not talking about one man for a few months, I'm talking about the entire institution of liberalism for nearly two decades.

PART TWO: THERE IS ONLY THE FIGHT, THE TACTICS OF OPPRESSIVE LEFTISTS

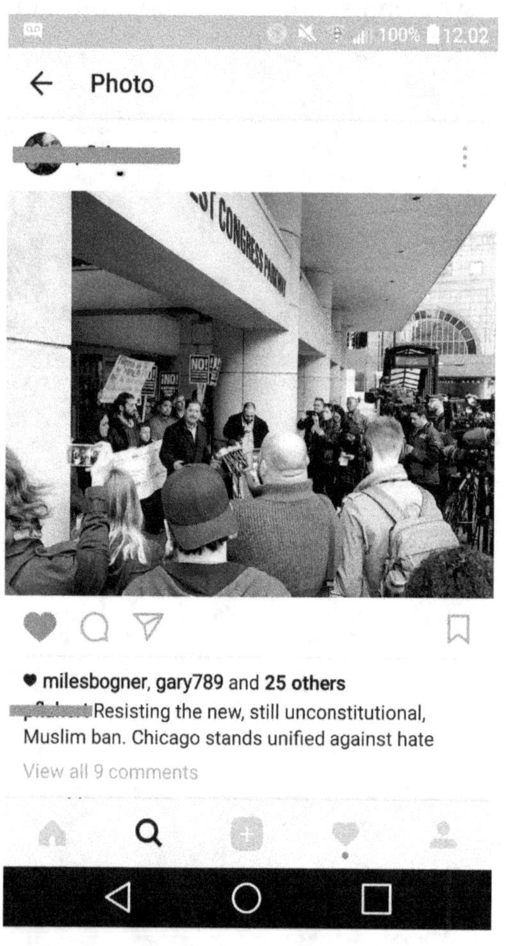

It was my intention to get this post out of the way last week, but life happened. I also couldn't really coherently give an honest perspective as I was "woke" to the many great moderate and conservative minds that a liberal media and intelligentsia had marginalized by virtue of their divergent opinions from the establishment. There was much to learn. After considering many angles, I settled upon the evolution of community organizing movement by the flawed absolutist ideologies of academia and the bitter argument it eventually caused with my brother's girlfriend, a community organizer, about a month ago when she protested a "Muslim Ban," which didn't pass the courts. The reason it did not pass should have been illegal, as the basis for the decision was Trump's character instead of the legality of the measures of his executive action. Al Jazeera says as much.

I'm not sure if her actual job title is community organizer, union organizer, union manager, protest organizer, or some combination I couldn't invent in my wildest dreams that includes cis gendered female, but she is tacitly of the left, a true leftist who has worked in unions and protests her entire life and eventually came so close to calling me a racist that I don't feel bad in the slightest calling her out, but won't divulge her name due to the family dispute trolling of her account would decidedly cause. While she doesn't make six figures, she makes a comfortable salary fighting perceived injustices. She is what I would call an extreme leftist. This is how our argument began on Instagram...

← **Comments**

Resisting the new, still unconstitu
al, Muslim ban. Chicago stands unified ag
hate

3d

jesseblogner Maybe a bit overstated?

2d   Reply

@jesseblogner are you
serious?

2d   Reply

jesseblogner Its not a muslim ban. 90%
of the muslims in the world are excluded. All these countries are enemies of
the united states. I really don't understand the controversy other than not
going through proper channels which
post LBJ presidents have all ignored.

2d   Reply

…If you want to skip my esoteric, but fascinating examination of the intellectual forces behind modern politics and see the conclusion, you're more than welcome to scroll down to the end.

Since it may cause confusion, I'm going to give a rough designation of terms. *Liberals* are people who vote for the Democratic party in all instances. They may be advocates of free speech. They can even have a libertarian streak and support Israel. However, in spite of the fact there are very rational liberals, the term includes all Democrats, essentially anyone left of center. For my purposes, I'm talking about moderate liberals like Bill Clinton in the 90s, JFK, FDR, Steven Spielberg, Sam Harris, Martin Luther King, Dave Rubin, maybe Bill Maher. I say maybe Bill Maher, because he and other classical liberals are beginning to embrace socialism.

Leftists are socialists who usually have extreme points of views and tactics that are meant to quiet any opposition. When science or economic reality opposes their narratives, they attack the enemy to misdirect them. They are disciples of community organizing movements invented by Saul Alinsky. While it's confusing to group Hillary Clinton and Barack Obama into this camp, Obama was a community organizer greatly influenced by extremists like Bill Ayres and Reverend Jeremiah Wright in his personal life and the works of Edward Said, who he shared a table with at least once at an extravagant fundraising dinner. The irony of socialists and their culinary sophistication.

While the media portrays Hillary as a moderate, Hillary Clinton's senior thesis at Wellesley was entitled "There is only the fight…: An Analysis of the Alinsky Model," you know the community organizer guy. John Podesta and George Soros follow the Alinsky model in their ill-fated attempt to control American politics in order build a globalist society without borders. Leftists now control the Democratic party, the intellectuals, mainstream culture and mainstream media excepting Fox. To combat stories that are favorable to the right, Soros has built alliances with leftist journalists for years and funded Media Matters, an Alinsky style far left fake news site mainly functioning as a place to discredit right wing journalism often cited by the mainstream media.

Leftists generally have little regard for America, as they see the thirteen colonies who escaped tyranny as an Imperial power that can never be forgiven for the genocide of Indians and slavery. I do sympathize with Native Americans on this issue, but it does not make me discount the vastly wonderful things America and capitalism has done, such as eradicating much of the world's hunger indirectly. In the leftist view, much like the refugee state of Israel, America's success means it was stolen. As Ben Shapiro notes about Bernie Sanders, "He sees somebody in a room with five dollars and somebody with one and he immediately says the guy with five dollars must have stolen something from the guy with one dollar."

In foreign policy, leftists always side with the underdog. Their hatred of even moderate nationalism and Imperialism (even in cases where the narrative is pure fiction) makes liberals side with some bad hombres. Leftists believe in cultural relativism, an anthropological approach which eventuated the ubiquitous belief that all non-white cultures implicitly have more or at least equal merit to Western cultures. They ignore the billions of people whose lives have been improved by liberal democracy. This is the genesis of the insanity you see on campuses today.

They may believe in Democracy, as long as Democracy is intended to benefit minorities, the transgendered and women above others. If they don't believe in Marxist theory, they general believe in the welfare state and cultural Marxism, the ideas of The Frankfurt School, a group of hugely influential German philosophers who left Nazi Germany and found American capitalism distasteful.

While I sympathize with many of their positions in a vacuum, the Frankfurt School's pessimistic view of American society in the 1940s and 1950s (I view America in that time period as one of the great eras in human history in technological innovation, education and the arts) is to me quite troubling when combined with the notions of cultural relativism. While I do not suggest it was The Frankfurt School's intention to impede on free speech and the free exchange of ideas, by separating societies into the two main classes of victim and oppressor, the following narrative prevailed.

Victim oppressor narratives create a system of multicultural tribalism that has infected young academics and turned them into something not unlike the totalitarian powers their work aimed to refute. When liberal public policy proves to only intensify the inequity between ethnicities, arguments against social welfare (aside from the Denmark-Norway-Sweden argument, countries whose combined population is equal to the New York Metropolitan Area flush with natural resources and until recently with Protestant work ethic) are put down by attacking the "oppressor" as a bigot.

This is the "no skin in the game" problem, Nassim Taleb, one of a handful of people who predicted the 2008 financial crisis and one of a handful of public intellectuals who publicly supported Trump speaks of. People become a lot less absolutist and theoretical when their lives are at risk. Academics are hugely influential in shaping the majority opinion of the ruling class with no risk to themselves, teaching five hours a week making six figures and taking five months off to "research," or ostensibly do whatever they want. If you don't agree with my assessment of the intellectual class, look at Karl Marx writing absolutist economic principles based on social structures that became the foundation for the Soviet Revolution and nearly a century of suffering, hunger and mass extermination of dissenters.

A less famous example of an intellectual altering the course of the world is Leo Strauss. Born into an Orthodox Jewish household, he evacuated Nazi Germany as a young scholar. Though a contemporary of the Frankfurt School thinkers, Strauss came to wildly different conclusions when he too embraced secularism and came to the similar conclusion that democracy's fatal flaw is that individualism would lead to nihilism. Strauss didn't divide the world into victim and oppressor, but philosophers and everyone else. The philosophers became political strategists. They were responsible for maintaining national security and myth-building, sometimes in the form of bizarre myths painting the picture of America's destiny to triumph over evil-doers and UFOs.

Pessimistic is a kind word for his Old Testament view of human nature in which, "The Philosophers need to tell noble lies not only to the people at large, but also to powerful politicians…in order to keep the ignorant masses in line." He accepted the inevitable unfairness of life and knew the only remedy was unity, a shared purpose. If the better world was based on myth, did it make the better world any less real?

Strauss' students used their professor's belief system to create neoconservatism, clearly the most influential political philosophy in the late-era deep state Cold War through the war in Iraq. These philosophers were to rule through vessels, famous men with charisma who spoke with gravitas, like Ronald Reagan, and empty vessels with name recognition whose fathers were already president, like George W. Bush. Strauss' ideas and politicians like

Paul Wolfowitz, Dick Cheney and Donald Rumsfeld were implementing anti-utopian ideology in the form airstrikes, coups, wars and nation building. While their policies were mired in failure after Iraq, they admirably believed they could form a better world. Strauss never had name-recognition in the era of the intellectual celebrity, but his work had more impact on America than any of his contemporaries. They ultimately failed because of their ignorance of the Middle East, but they were not evil warmongers. They had ideals that they believed could be the savior of a crumbling world, a corrupt world that looks quaint in the splintered society we now exist in.

By all indications Hillary Clinton wanted a mix of Kissinger style globalists and good vs. evil neocons in her administration. This could have created some insane mix of politically correct Cultural Marxism on the edges of totalitarianism, open borders, aggressive wars in the Middle East and a possible reigniting of the Cold War. Or it could have been the stabilizing force, wherein the smartest men in the room could reevaluate the errors of the past overseas.

Saul Alinsky, like Strauss was an ex Orthodox Jew aiming to bring an opposing theory into practice. The endlessly charismatic man made real social progress by fighting those who went against his protests by characterizing his detractors as well as neutral parties to them as an evil opposition. While we champion Martin Luther King's nonviolent resistance, guys like Alinsky were attacking the power structures behind the scenes by demonizing detractors of progressive politics as simpletons and bigots. In Alinsky's view, "The job of the organizer is to maneuver and bait the establishment so that it will publicly attack him as a 'dangerous enemy.'"

We see the same strategies today, in a world where all races and ethnicities have the same legal rights as everyone else. Like terrorism, our enemy is not easily identifiable. It's called racism and when that doesn't track, there's phantom terrorism that some call unconscious prejudice. To combat the tribalist instincts of humanity, the liberals have brilliantly devised the strategy of making words less offensive and helping you find your hidden prejudices you probably aren't even aware of, to make certain your lack of prejudice doesn't stop you from grouping people by race and ethnicity. According to leftists, opposition to this way of thinking is assumed to be racism, just as it was racist to oppose Barack Obama. Tell that to the ingenious black conservative economist Thomas Sowell, who calls Barack Obama the worst president in US history without any doubts.

Ask yourself, is it socially acceptable for an Upper Middle Class person to support Trump? Is it OK to be critical of Barack Obama's foreign policy?

Unless you follow extremist politics pretty closely, you probably first heard the job title "community organizer" when Obama was taking down Hillary in the primaries in 2007. The job title sounds about as fishy as Bachelor contestants claiming to be an "Oil Trader," or a "Sport Fishing Enthusiast." As strange as it may sound (you may be having the why should I care thought as you're reading this, give it a second to simmer) in the 1930s, Saul Alinsky, who only right-wing conspiracy theorists, the Barack & Alec Baldwin crowd seem to care about, devised the community organizing movement ostensibly to give those without power a voice in the zeitgeist.

David Horowitz, the Marxist Huey Newton confidante turned conservative thinker gets to the core ideology of our last administration in his pamphlet, "Barack Obama's Rules for

Revolution. The Alinsky Model." He writes, "The strategy of working within the system until you can accumulate enough power to destroy it was what '60s radicals called 'boring from within.' … Like termites, they set about to eat away at the foundations of the building in expectation that one day they could cause it to collapse."

While there are curiously no large anti-war rallies, social protest has amped up since the Tea Party and Occupy Movement, culminating in a large-scale continual protest of Donald Trump. The media is complicit in its attack of Trump, pointing to a conspiracy that Trump and The Kremlin rigged the elections. The left claims post-truth politics belongs to the right, which is simply not the case. Mainstream news outlets like The New York Times and CNN are no longer different than Info Wars, spending inordinate amounts of time speculating on Trump and Bannon's actual intentions without a shred of evidence. Never mind how underreported it is that Obama was spying on Trump's administration, according to Bloomberg. Salon and others like the New York Times go to great lengths to discredit actual Watergate-style scandals of the Obama White House while they cling to the hope they can prove collusion between Trump and Russia with no real evidence. There doesn't even seem to be evidence that Russia hacked the DNC, which all mainstream news outlets reported as fact.

One example of an irrational conspiracy theorist, who the left trusts without reservation is Rachel Maddow. She embarrassed herself by proclaiming with a stolen tax return that Donald Trump made about 150 million dollars in 2005 and paid an effective rate of 24%, about as much as Tim Kaine and nearly triple Mitt Romney. Rachel Maddow is either playing 4-D chess (she knows something we don't), or is just not all that bright. I would assume the latter. Maddow is the perfect encapsulation of the Democratic Party

Media Complex. She lives in the Alinsky bubble.

Since I am not an institution, I think it is OK for me to follow their lead. Right here, I'm going to introduce another conspiracy. My thought is on Bannon's recommendation Trump supports Russia, because he believes The Middle East will become more stable under the rule of secular dictatorships than Sharia states. Devoid of religious dogma, the Middle East does become more predictable at the very least.

Clearly it is no longer acceptable for the left to consider the right's position on any issue. Even Maher, who is highly critical of Islam, will never defend things like "The Muslim Ban," in spite of his personal position. Maher is still clinging to the value of institutions and can't wrap his head around the idea that all these Trump/Russia conspiracies are speculative, including the intonations of the real story of Trump campaign manager Paul Manafort's ten-million-dollar salary from a Putin ally in the Ukraine. Hillary's campaign manager John Podesta may have eerily similar conflicts of interest. Where there's smoke there doesn't seem to be any concrete evidence. Though her banner read, "More Than Circumstantial," which shouldn't be a surprise on a News Network, all I saw was circumstantial evidence in relation to Trump's campaign.

Democracy is being compromised by Republicans shaken by the accusations of letting people die and being racists. Conservatives cannot present their ideology in the service of discourse. Liberals have been forced to use the totalitarian leftist methods, simply because, as William F Buckley proclaimed half a century ago, "Liberals claim to want to give a hearing to other views, but then are shocked and offended to discover that there are other views." Bill Maher, after pretending to be a libertarian, as a big defender of institutions like partisan papers, he hypocritically explains why it is moronic to be right of center in this climate. He is claiming idleness creates apolitical conservatives, without evidence other than the badmouthing of liberals who believe they are more evolved than conservatives, because they are of the pseudo-intellectual class.

Liberals see Maher as some sort of intellectual titan. He is undoubtedly intelligent, but I see something not unlike the fool of Tolstoy's *Anna Karenina,* Stepan Arkadyevitch. "Stepan Arkadyevitch had not chosen his political opinions or his views; these political opinions and views had come to him of themselves, just as he did not choose the shapes of his hat and coat, but simply took those that were being worn…If there was a reason for his preferring liberal to conservative views, which were held also by many of his circle, it arose not from his considering liberalism more rational, but from its being in closer accordance with his manner of life. The liberal party said that in Russia everything is wrong, and certainly Stepan Arkadyevitch had many debts and was decidedly short of money. The liberal party said that marriage is an institution quite out of date, and that it needs reconstruction; and family life certainly afforded Stepan Arkadyevitch little gratification, and forced him into lying and hypocrisy, which was so repulsive to his nature. The liberal party said, or rather allowed it to be understood, that religion is only a curb to keep in check the barbarous classes of the people… and he liked his newspaper, as he did his cigar after dinner, for the slight fog it diffused in his brain."

There are very real reasons to be concerned about a Trump administration, particularly Trump's word being worth very little. Democracy cannot function without two sides working with agreed upon facts. This is why democracy hasn't functioned very well since a few months after 9/11. Both sides have lost credibility, including bedrocks of formerly falsifiable news organizations.

While it is encouraging that Trump tends to be right more than he is wrong, if he were to keep his mouth shut from time to time his administration would actually be flourishing. He hires great people and destroys mostly useless government programs. It is not great for Trump, but still, the alternative was a lot worse.

Below, I lose my temper at my brother (in purplish blue and blue blue) and his girlfriend (in red) below for making leftist arguments that made it very clear that supporting Trump over Hillary was a no brainer in spite of the conventional wisdom.

← **Comments**

@jesseblogner Even homeland security released a report stating that the travel ban will be ineffective. They found the majority of people in the united states inspired by terrorists were actually US citizens who felt rejected and persecuted. The travel ban will only make this worse. The others came from 26 different countries and country of origin was found to have almost no predictive value. Virtually no one came from the countries banned. It is a hate and fear filled policy. Just think about how similar it is to how America turned away Jews during WWII because of antisemitism and a fear that NAZI spies could sneak in.

2d Reply

← **Comments**

How many refugees have carried out terrorist attacks in the us recently? Zero. https://www.google.com/amp/s/amp.cnn.com/cnn/2017/01/29/us/refugee-terrorism-trnd/index.html. And how many racists will feel further emboldened to commit hate crimes against (assumed) muslims because of trumps callous approach? Uncertain, but We're already off to a good start there. But yeah, you're right, if more people knew about the ramifications of this ban on national security they would certainly be more afraid of the positive recruiting effect it will have on isis as they can more definitively claim that America hates all muslims.

2d Reply

Comments
jesseblogner ( ) I know you're too smart to think there is any equivalency between the Jews of the Holocaust. There are 50 muslim majority states. There was no Jewish state. Large swathes of Muslims in Europe and, hasn't elected anyone who acknowledges the existence of the holocaust. The paris and brussels attackers used refugee routes. I don't know why you would trust an unelected government agency like the dhs that didn't acknowledge radical islam or jihad last year on its website and has been selling the same bullshit sleeper cells theory since the bush ad-ministration. The threat is more likely to be from syria than the us. Sorry.
2d   Reply

jesseblogner The full comment was condensed. Dont know why. It was saying that many refugees in europe believe in sharia, support jihad and are responsible for huge spikes in rape. The holocaust comment was about iran, which produces great filmmakers and rampant holocaust denial.
Add a comment...

After being genuinely disturbed by my own flesh and blood's insistence that Radical Islam was no threat to the world, I tried to reason with the left (my brother and his girlfriend). The third part of this series will be how my pleading for the left to consider how blind allegiance with conservative Islam is aiding in oppression at home and overseas. This rationale led me to be called something close to a bigot after a long back and forth on Facebook. This party line of the left fueled my fire to publicly support Trump, who I believe is far less dangerous than the politically correct leftist movement.

Rather than continue to stoke the fire, the conclusion of the final installment in this series, which will be revealed in the coming weeks will be looking towards solutions. After outlining the mess of American politics, I believe (as is the way of news and blogging) presenting huge problems without offering solutions is fundamentally useless. Everything is malleable, including the dictatorial power of radical Islamists in the Middle East and a broken democratic system. You, the citizens have the real power, but you don't know how to use it against a right wing that appears to have fascist tendencies and a left wing that does have fascist tendencies. Believe it or not, I do have constructive ideas for our uncertain times. The ball is in your court.

PART THREE: BUILDING A WORLD OF LOVE OUT OF THE ASHES

(White House May 4th, 2017, American and Palestinian Flag: Wikipedia Commons)

If you're squeamish, feel free to skip the 3rd paragraph. It is about genital mutilation.

Ayaan Hirsi Ali's father, Hirsi Magan Isse, didn't believe in female genital mutilation. In Ali's homeland of Somalia, 98% of young girls undergo the ritual. In other more moderate coastal African countries including Egypt, this rite is performed for 91% percent of women. An elite dissident, Ali's father was too dangerous to the newly installed government to live freely in his homeland. When he was jailed, the three-year-old Ali was left in the care of her grandmother. Since "Uncircumcised girls will be possessed by devils, fall into vice and perdition, and become whores," the reasonable thing was done, her genitals were cut out.

The procedure goes as follows. "After the child's clitoris and labia are carved out, scraped off, or, in more compassionate areas, merely cut or pricked, the whole area is often sewn up, so that a thick band of tissue forms a chastity belt made of the girl's own scarred flesh. A small hole is carefully situated to permit a thin flow of pee…Many girls die during or after their excision, from infection." This practice is beginning to make its way to America.

A few years later, Ali and her father later escaped to Saudi Arabia, before settling in Kenya. As a teenager, Ali embraced the ideology of the Muslim Brotherhood. She decided to wear a hijab, a fairly radical sartorial choice in early 80s Africa. Still, Ali's arranged marriage was enough motivation for her to begin to question her faith and seek asylum in the Netherlands in 1992 at the age of 23.

She quickly began to embrace Western society. After gaining awareness of the works of secular thinkers divorced from religion like Sigmund Freud, she could contemplate the luck of her situation in a free society. Her world was so isolated from the West, she had never heard of the Holocaust, but knew well the perceived evil of Zionism.

By the age of 33, she was a Member of the Dutch Parliament. During this time, she provided the voiceover for the short film *Submission*, depicting the punishments to women as described in the Quran, which pointedly warns the public about the widespread misguided attempts at literal interpretation of the religious text.

The filmmaker, Theo Van Gogh, was murdered. The attacker left a five-page death threat addressed to Ayaan pinned to Theo's chest by a dagger. Even after living under a fatwa in hiding, she vocally opposed Islamic oppression of women across the globe, using her experience to expose horrors the West was largely ignorant of in her landmark memoir *Infidel: My Life*. Clearly, as someone who actively works to combat the oppression of women in Africa and the Middle East like herself, she should be a feminist icon.

Curiously, in some circles, the exact opposite has held true. The Brooklyn born Conservative Muslim Women's March leading hipster prop of Bernie Sanders, The Muslim Brotherhood and the Democratic Party, Linda Sarsour, has attacked Ali relentlessly. I only found one critical liberal (i.e. mainstream) Op-Ed about Sarsour, in spite of the fact she advocates for Sharia law and shouted about the evils of Charlie Hebdo days after the attack, while supporting The Muslim Brotherhood and the theocratic terrorist party of her native Palestine Hamas, that was formed with the aid of the Muslim Brotherhood. Even in Brooklyn, her marriage was arranged. Though her sect only allows men to decide on the issues of abortion, she felt it perfectly reasonable to announce the Women's March would have to exclude half the women in America who oppose abortion.

Brigitte Gabriel= Ayaan Hirsi Ali. She's asking 4 an a$$ whippin'. I wish I could take their vaginas away - they don't deserve to be women.

3/8/11, 22:38

While Ayaan Hirsi Ali visits Bill Maher and Anderson Cooper from time to time, her message is largely ignored by the leftist majority of the mainstream media. Fox News rightly champions her expertise and heroism, but this only further marginalizes her voice in the culture, since liberals who dominate most if not all mainstream culture view Fox and even the never-Trump voices of the Wall Street Journal as sensationalist fake news. The left doesn't have any use for Ayaan Hirsi Ali, because she contradicts the false Islam as religion of peace narrative. Linda Sarsour is to speak at the City University of New York commencement next month, to further con young people into the belief that there is no moral justification to support Israel who she calls White Supremacists, though 65% of Israel is non-white (to be clear the 3.2 million Middle Eastern, Central Asian and Northern African Jews are classified as white in America and Europe, though they have negligible differences in DNA and pigmentation to Middle Eastern Arabs, who are classified as minorities).

Leftists generally side with the oppressed, in the victim-oppressor paradigm. Still, party loyalty trumps moral authority. Andrew Breitbart became aware of this hypocrisy watching the womanizer lush Ted Kennedy "of Chappaquiddick fame" and Joe Biden relentlessly attack the black conservative Supreme Court Justice, Clarence Thomas, for allegedly "talking about sex and pornography?" In hindsight, even the accusations presented without evidence are much tamer than one would assume lawyers, judges and politicians discuss if you've ever watched an episode of *Veep*.

This made it clear that ideology matters more than race. The press skewered Thomas as a perverted misogynist, while Bill Clinton was celebrated by the media in the preceding years as a breath of fresh air, with a sexual history as sordid as Caligula. Just like the left, the right will side with completely with moronic views in service of party loyalty from time to time, but they don't have the weapon of the race card, or the "you're a racist" card to end the discussion. The only defense to the attack on Western values is Donald Trump.

When Israel miraculously began winning wars on multiple fronts in 1967, to the left, they began to resemble the West. Before the state was established, England promised the territory to both the secular Zionists, who rightfully escaped religious persecution and the Arab nobility of Jerusalem who wanted to form a caliphate. During the Holocaust, with nowhere to go, Jews arrived by ships and battled The British navy and Arabs to find a safe haven. Thousands died. This was remedied by Churchill, when Israel became a state in 1948.

A year earlier, when Britain decided to leave Palestine, The Arab leaders wouldn't agree to Israel taking 56% of the area that now compromises Israel, The West Bank and Gaza. The fact that this state is much smaller than Israel (even by the absurd UN orders) is forgotten by many, like the man behind the decision to reject the idea.

The Grand Mufti Amin al-Husseini, the genetically Caucasian noble of Jerusalem who traced his roots all the way to Mohammed was an honorary Aryan, worked in anti-Semitic Nazi propaganda after having developed a knack for it in the 20s when he devised the idea of Palestinian statehood in opposition to the Zionists. Of course he would be King in this vision. In his first meeting with Adolf Hitler in 1941, the Mufti requested the Fuhrer's help in their common enemy, the Jews, but Hitler saw it as a fool's errand. He knew there was no united people living in Palestine. The Mufti's belief that he could destroy the Jews and take the land for himself is what created this situation, along with Jordan's fearfulness of a Palestinian State and unwillingness to absorb the Arabs of the region.

Though on all sides except for Jordan (for the most part) historically, Israel has been surrounded by enemies and the Jews had nowhere to go during and after enduring the Holocaust, they are viewed as oppressors. I don't see the damage in allowing Jews to settle what was then sparsely populated land, after the Holocaust made it pretty clear they weren't safe in Europe.

The backlash reminds me of our current climate with the Syrian refugee non-debate. Universal hatred of Israel in the Middle East and North Africa forced massive expulsion of Jews into Israel. While they coexisted in the Muslim countries, Jews were treated as second class citizens. Of the 75,000 Jews in Egypt, only 10,000 were citizens. Though there were only hundreds of reported deaths, nearly a million Jews of Arabic descent were expelled from their homes and sent on an exodus to Israel from Muslim nations.

Unlike many of the powerful Arab powers of the day, Israel absorbed the refugees without question. Though it may seem tribal to leftists, the largely secular Zionists felt it was their duty to take in those who they shared a heritage with in spite of their wildly different cultures. The refugee state of Israel, constantly under attack to this very day by powerful Arab countries and the Palestinians became emblematic of Western Imperialism.

Today's world is lacking in core values, so we live in the confusion of moral relativism, where the level of victimhood takes precedence over the values a culture holds. The worse the values, the less responsibility the nation has to justify its actions. When the UN puts Saudi Arabia on the Women's Rights Commission, it's hard to take the globalist leaders seriously. Since Israel is a liberal democracy that began with the migration of Europeans before the Holocaust, the very right of the nation to exist is in question, even though Western Europeans make up barely 100,000 of the country's six million citizens.

No one on either side wants to exist in reality. Levels of victimhood determine the value of arguments, whether the argument is valid or not. Self-proclaimed "victims" like Sarsour who hold objectively terrifying points of view that directly contradict once universal liberal values are sanctified, while those who fight real injustice are ignored or even criticized.

Weighing the insanity of the left's decision to treat Islam like every other religion and after fighting with my brother and his girlfriend about the ultimately unsuccessful "Muslim Ban," that excluded 88% of the world's Muslims on Instagram, I took to Facebook, to embed video evidence that I had not lost my mind. I wasn't paranoid or hateful.

Jesse Bogner shared a link — with ~~Rhonda Trajkoski Flaherty~~ and Miles Bogner.

March 8 at 1:08am · © ▾

Bill Maher to Ayaan Hirsi Ali: Why Do Liberals 'Blame the Victim' When It Comes to Islam?

YOUTUBE.COM

👍 Like   💬 Comment   ➦ Share

👍 Seth Bogner and Gole Trajkoski

Jesse Bogner https://www.youtube.com/watch?v=sQGLoAV5zWM on somalia

Like · Reply · ◐ 1 · March 8 at 12:17am · Edited

Jesse Bogner https://www.youtube.com/watch?v=HqWJZW-u85k fundamental flaws in muslim theology in muslim majority countries and how to deal with immigration and find ways to help syrian refugees

Ayaan Hirsi Ali on How to Fight Islamic Extremism

YOUTUBE.COM

Like · Reply · Remove Preview · ◐ 1 · March 8 at 12:31am · Edited

I got the typically thoughtless emotional responses of a community organizer. Rather than examine the inherent danger of bringing in Syrian refugees, I was talked down to like a redneck Trump supporter. So, I cited my protestations with my brother's girlfriend's conventional multicultural wisdom.

While I'm sure people will misconstrue my point as I'm wrestling with a sensitive issue and the leftist perspective on these matters is that it's racist for the white man to examine them, I have no problem doing so because I know I have no hate in my heart for anyone but evil theocratic governments.

As a spiritual Jewish person, I care about freedom of religion, but believe it's dangerous to freely admit people from oppressive cultures while signaling that since Islam is a universally beautiful religion of peace, everything is kosher. Hillary with her world without borders, leftist message with some neoconservatism spliced in was saying, "We understand why you hate the West, that it is totally fine for refugees from Somalia, Syria and other incredibly problematic nations, you know to advocate for sharia and treat women as one-half a person. We're totally cool with that man, cause you know, you can't judge the merits of such a beautiful culture." But why can't you judge?

The left judges all the time. Dark-skinned Imams, religious Kings and oligarchs controlled by Imams are usually beyond critique, but secular Syrians like Assad who look like White European dictators are clearly Nazis. Like Trump's decision to reverse his plan on Syria, the leftists are guided by emotion more than results. Like the neocons, they've adopted the "if someone looks like the bad guy in a movie we go after him strategy."

How can you solve a problem without looking at the details rationally? You can't just throw money at it. This isn't Keynesian economics (which I don't really buy), it's life and death. The future of the Western World, the place that brought you everything from Aristotle to Game of Thrones and most other things in your life, is at stake. The left says it's obvious that Western values need to be demystified, as culture has no inherent value. I just want to remove the protective barrier that disallows us from addressing these problems aloud, because we're asking a very serious question here. We're asking if Western civilization is worth saving.

On the right, you shouldn't accept that the United States is some sort of flawless monolith of good, fighting pure evil above critique, and the left shouldn't trust that America is the most evil empire in the history of the world, "cause…The Indians, I mean Native Americans and neoliberalism man."

"What is neoliberalism?"

"I don't know man, less restrictions on the banks. More collusion between government and banking, ensuring that the banks benefit more than the middle class."

"Oh, OK, I see what you mean. Though I'm a free market capitalist, the banks need some restrictions to protect themselves from their own greed."

"I just think the banks have too much power, like a private corporation shouldn't be too big to fail." This is the kind of dialogue liberal and conservative stoner teenagers should be having. While I wish they weren't so high, it's valuable for them to see the merits in each other's argument. If they weren't so high they would probably remember to research more perspectives from reputable sources to check their stance. When people have basic literacy of government issues from different perspectives they can debate and develop valuable opinions.

Without checks and balances between the parties, in education and the media, young and even some older liberals sound like the Stasi. Like government, people just attack the other side, rarely thinking about their worldview's implications. I don't love the West's foreign policy post World War 2, but I don't understand how it makes me a right-wing lunatic in the eyes of some when I say to grown men that, "We are not as bad as the terrorists and it's not even close. I've actually thought about this. Just because I don't take Howard Zinn and Noam Chomsky at face value, doesn't mean I like fascism. How old are you, 18?"

The argument below has my answers in (). She clearly doesn't answer my factual, reasoned arguments, because liberals are not used to dealing with informed opposition and when their arguments don't stick, they attack the character of the opponent so they don't have to win losing battles.

-Bill mahr is an islamophobic asshole
-Every orthodox religion has oppressive doctrine.
- Every religion can be manipulated to incite hatred and violence.
-Islam, like every other religion or other grouping, is not monolithic.
- what you've posted makes it seem like you are arguing for vetting based on religion, because you disagree with the tenants of that religion.
-It's simply the right thing to do to take in refugees whose lives are at risk, especially considering how our country played a huge role in creating the instability they are fleeing.
-The people who are desecrating Jewish cemeteries and drawing swastikas on synagogues are citing the same arguments you've been using all day, arguments based in hatred and fear.
- here, muslims and Jews are uniting against trump inspired hatred and violence to support and protect each other.

Like · Reply · 1 · March 8 at 1:32am

Jesse Bogner -Bill mahr is an islamophobic asshole (islamophobic is a catch all word that denies someone the right to talk about islam rationally. if you say that culture in muslim majority states is oppressive, i think that counts as islamophobic. islam post the 1970s is often an "infallible" political ideology as much as a religion.)
-Every orthodox religion has oppressive doctrine. (not to the same extent. if you're talking about orthodox judaism "the oppression" is entirely voluntary, you aren't killed or stoned for things like adultery and leaving the religion and no one imposes their values on others. it's completely incomparable and you know that.)
- Every religion can be manipulated to incite hatred and violence. (islam is often used to incite hatred and violence. judaism, not so much. i can think of one religiously fueled major terrorist attack by an orthodox jew, baruch goldstein in response to the oslo accords. there are maybe a few hundred lunatics who explicitly support his actions, implicitly maybe a few thousand. with islam, this is in the tens of millions explicitly, implicity at least 100 million as a very conservative estimate, it could be half a billion)

billion)
-Islam, like every other religion or other grouping, is not monolithic. (i never said it was. i'm a fan of sufism generally. but the leadership of the major islam states are largely religious zealots or dictators. these dangerous ideologies are brainwashed into the population with state controlled media and education. the shia states which are more moderate on things like women's rights invented suicide bombing in the 70s (using their poor children to clear landmines in iran and syria which were once cultural bastions) while the sunni leaders are now mostly exclusively wahabbist, because saudi arabia has spent billions of dollars promoting the ideology all over the middle east, in europe and now in america. this is the literal interpretation of the qu'ran that influenced bin laden, the return to the past)
- what you've posted makes it seem like you are arguing for vetting based on religion, because you disagree with the tenants of that religion. (of course you should vet people coming from countries with large fractions of religious extremists who support jihad and want sharia law)
-It's simply the right thing to do to take in refugees whose lives are at risk, especially considering how our country played a huge role in creating the instability they are fleeing. (it would be better to fix the problem in syria than take in refugees. also i think it would make more sense for the gulf states to take in said refugees as they share a culture and language and are geographically more accessible. never mind they are gigantic, rich states. if we do, which i think would be great, it would require serious therapy and education)
-The people who are desecrating Jewish cemeteries and drawing swastikas on synagogues are citing the same arguments you've been using all day, arguments based in hatred and fear. (this isn't hatred and fear. this is reality. i don't hate muslims. i love everyone. in israel a lot of muslims agree with these stances, many because they have lived through brainwashing and bullshit oppressive ideology. by blindly accepting islam wholesale you are supporting widespread oppression. in "moderate countries" like egypt 90% of women are circumcised. i just think if you take in millions of refugees you will be surprised at the horrible implications. look at detroit, which has become a breeding ground for islamic extremism. BTW, the JCC bombings, we don't know who made them. never mind the one person they found to have done it who is a huge liberal, an ex intercept journalist. it wouldn't surprise me if george soros was behind a lot of it to make trump look bad.)

I couldn't have predicted better, with the last parenthesis of my post as the JCC bomb threats were done by a mentally unstable Israeli teenager and an ex-Intercept (apparently also mentally ill) reporter trying to get back at his Jewish ex-girlfriend in some roundabout delusional way. It was obviously clear to me that the extremism and hatred was coming from left with much more force than the right and that hellholes like Detroit were becoming *Escape From New York* style dystopias of alternate societies of Muslim extremism bent on bringing us back to the dark ages, like the cliterectomy stories coming from there seem to suggest.

Then I was very wrong about the following, as Trump has become a neocon, I believe to salvage his unpopularity and show he's not Putin's lapdog to the conspiratorial mainstream media. This isn't working as much as I'm sure Trump predicted, but if he remembers he was elected because he was the antithesis of Killary, everything should be OK in time. He shouldn't worry about his popularity since the left doesn't have any candidates worth their salt.

 **Jesse Bogner** https://theintercept.com/.../the-new-yorkers-big-cover.../ Hillary Clinton, however, had a much different view of all this. She was often critical of Obama's refusal to pursue aggression and belligerence in his foreign policy, particularly in Syria, where she and her closest allies wanted to impose a no-fly zone, be more active in facilitating regime change, and risk confrontation with Russia there. The New Yorker article describes the plight of Evelyn Farkas, the Obama Pentagon's senior Russia adviser who became extremely frustrated by Obama's refusal to stand up to Putin over Ukraine but was so relieved to learn that Clinton, as president, would do so:

The Russian experts heralded by the article also feared that Clinton — in contrast to Obama — was so eager for escalated U.S. military action in Syria to remove Assad that a military conflict with Russia was a real possibility:

It's impossible to overstate how serious of a risk this was. Recall that one of Clinton's most vocal surrogates, former acting CIA chief Michael Morell, explicitly said — in a Dr. Strangelove-level creepy video — that he wanted to kill not only Iranians and Syrians but also Russians in Syria.

The New Yorker's Big Cover Story Reveals Five Uncomfortable Truths...

THEINTERCEPT.COM | BY GLENN GREENWALD

Like · Reply · Remove Preview · March 8 at 3:44am · Edited

 **Jesse Bogner** https://www.youtube.com/watch?v=-lvt2NmbyGg

"I want to scare Assad" Mike Morell (Aug 8, 2016) |...

YOUTUBE.COM

Like · Reply · Remove Preview · March 8 at 3:40am

Here is the moment it was clear to me I was a conservative. When I saw that video on Glenn Greenwald's uncommonly impartial post for someone in the current media landscape (especially for someone to the left of Jane Fonda) on the really interesting 13,000 word (more than twice as long as this, if you can believe it) Trump Russia collusion New Yorker piece, it was clear I could no longer be a Democrat.

When someone who knows me pretty well calls me hateful and full of fear, for not supporting a candidate driven by hate, fear and corruption, it was over. I could no longer look at reality from that side of the aisle. My maybe a bit brash point of view about the Muslim world was rejected without consideration, because leftists are ideologues.

Of course this isn't an assault on the majority of Muslims and not individual Muslims who by and large are some of the most interesting people I know (I'm sure this statement will be construed as racist by someone), but political ideologies dependent on the Quran, and its political aim to turn the map green from Rome to Constantinople, is now sacred territory that cannot be touched. This is in spite of the fact that the ultra-rich Saudis (3rd biggest military budget on the planet, almost double Russia) and the people they're recruiting seem to be doing a good job fulfilling their aims. With the world less dependent on Saudi oil, they could see the time to strike as sooner than later. It bothers me that the left with all their political activism never examines these issues. The premise is that they are always right, because they are morally superior. If America were to give up on the military, what would happen?

Everything I hated about multiculturalism, mass surveillance, the cold-shouldered acceptance of Israel as an ally (while Obama privately screwed Israel at every chance he could), political correctness, dividing people by ethnicities and inefficient welfare was now married to the inefficient warfare of neoconservatism. As unpredictable as Trump is and as angry at his administration I am over Syria, I could not support the clearly inequivalent forces of evil that Clinton aligned herself with to lose her campaign (both the Sunni extremists and the brownshirt social justice warriors).

While I don't think 600 Muslims polled is an accurate sample size to support the claim of the far right media that 51% of Muslims in America support sharia, I would assume our demographics resemble England where 23% want sharia and half think homosexuality should be illegal. Though Pew stopped polling on Sharia in America (probably in service of a PC agenda), they did find 8% of Muslims think suicide bombings are often or sometimes justified in defending Islam. While it's a fairly low number, that's 300,000 jihadist sympathizers living in America. 299,999 excluding Linda Sarsour. No wonder the surveillance net of the deep state is too wide to catch anyone.

According to the left, it's ignorant to blame immigration for terror. This is doubly true when it is responsible for the Brussels and Paris attacks, and a host of other terrorist attacks throughout Europe. Talking to a highly educated Swedish girl about Paris, she said it was OK, "because more people died immigrating to Europe than were killed in the attacks." If life were only a numbers game it would be a valid point, but academia is where wisdom goes to die. Like Chomsky, she completely ignores motivation. She hasn't even considered that Muslim extremism could harm Sweden, though it already has.

In Sweden, a country that has ironically made checkpoints at its borders to prevent undocumented immigration, it was made illegal to publicly advocate against accepting refugees, in spite of the fact roughly ¾ of the refugees are males, many young and single. Of course the place where civil liberties have been destroyed in favor of "tolerance" is the place the left idealizes.

This is the type of thing that is inappropriate to point out, just as it's politically incorrect to mention the widely held extreme theocratic Muslim beliefs to the tune of executing homosexuals in the cultural bastion Iran, honor killings in the oppressed Gaza and the raping of infidels in Germany, Iraq, Kurdistan and virtually every hotbed of Muslim extremism.

Cast to the side, women are unable to drive by law in Saudi Arabia. Even if a Saudi has four wives, none of them can drive to the grocery store. There are many women who enjoy wearing their burkas in such a place, and I'm sure many people are treated well interpersonally, but this involuntary theocratic modesty is the opposite of feminism.

Somehow it's OK for the Obama administration to sell 115 billion dollars of weapons there, while he and Hillary were fully aware that the Saudi government was funding ISIS. Even if the Wikileaks report where this was revealed was spurned by Russian intelligence (there is still not one credible shred of evidence to support this), it's an uncomfortable truth to reconcile. Curiously no one has denied the validity of Assange's leaks, while American intelligence agencies sling his name through the mud.

This revelation is of course why Obama was constantly underplaying the importance of ISIS, calling them JV, before saying ISIL (the name for combined ISIS and Al Qaeda forces), to appear less wrong about ISIS (if only to his administration), subtly projecting with the "L sound" that ISIS's newfound strength was the result of its allegiance with Al Qaeda, whose power was always grossly exaggerated by the federal government.

The 150 billion dollars Iran was given to not make nuclear weapons for ten years in hopes they would buy weapons from us has not worked out, since their weapons were purchased on the cheap from Russia, as we fight a proxy war with both powers in our pursuit of Assad who poses literally no threat to America, despite Hillary Clinton's insistence on reverting our foreign policy back to neoconservatism.

Trump fell into this trap. It was a great disappointment to me, as we're now fighting alongside Saudi Arabia. This is the same place where Osama bin Laden's dad, Mohammed bin Awad, fathered 56 children by 22 wives (only four at a time as prescribed by sharia). The right wing often cites single motherhood as the greatest predictor of crime, but I would venture a guess that Osama's criminal inclinations owed a larger debt to Wahhabi sect of Sunni Islam that the majority of Saudi Arabia practices. Scarier still to a Democrat, the guy's political philosophy was largely borrowed from Noam Chomsky. These ideas became Obama's speaking points.

If you are on the left, you may be wondering why one would diverge into Saudi Arabia, and 9/11, when talking about "The Muslim Ban." It's not to fear-monger and justify "Islamophobia (a totalitarian word)," but to illustrate the real root causes of terror. Saudi Arabia is the country that has spent more than 100 billion dollars exporting Sunni extremism throughout the Muslim World, Europe and even America over the past few decades, with other slightly less extreme jihadist groups like the Muslim Brotherhood following suit, wisely forging alliances with leftist political activists, so people like my brother and his girlfriend unconsciously associate Islam with Civil Rights and Planned Parenthood.

You might find David Horowitz's tactics below unseemly, but what he reveals below is the reality the leftists willfully ignore in favor of Sarsour and Bin Laden's point.

By and large, the majority of people in the Muslim world, like any other religion, are pretty apathetic about religion and jihad. Still, in my experience, most secular Muslims I know detest Israel, but this isn't different from many of my liberal friends. My concern is that according to a very low estimate, 133 million of the world's 1.6 billion Muslims believe in jihadist terror, a lot of whom believe it is justifiable to exterminate the Jews, especially what Sarsour once referred to as the "creepy Zionists." So if you want to compare Islam to Christianity, the parallels only exist if you're talking about the Spanish Inquisition of the 15th century.

It was pretty clear to me with America's ally Saudi Arabia omitted from the list this wasn't a Muslim ban. In Part 2, I wrote of the Hawaii judge's decision that he based largely on the speculation that since Donald Trump was Islamophobic and professed to ban Muslims on his campaign, it meant that the ban was unconstitutional, in its targeting of one religion. I don't believe speculation needs to play such a large role in our legal system. However, Trump probably should have presented a more reasoned plan for preventing terrorists and extremists from entering the United States. However, my fight had nothing to do with that.

My fight was with the endless accusations that everyone who disagreed with the Democrats on this issue and virtually any other issue was cast as a bigoted redneck, those who Hillary Clinton called irredeemable and deplorable.

As someone who grew up in elite circles, I understand how these things work. Upper Middle Class intellectuals and the extremely wealthy shape public opinion. When no politician in their right mind would bring up gay marriage and the legalization of marijuana (two positions I support btw), you could feel the visceral condescension of flyover country morality. The same thing is happening today with transgender issues, to devastating effect. It's now bigoted to critique small children getting hormone therapy, when most children who think they are transgender actually end up being happy homosexuals.

While the elites have little to no stake in the outcomes of their social policy perspectives, their egos are coddled by the belief that their deep sympathy for minorities makes them better people than the Christians and rednecks who have an irrational fear of God, women with penises in bathrooms with their small children, and immigrants.

Unlike Middle Class Americans, most elites have little interaction with other ethnicities aside from minority elites and employees. Working and Middle Class whites more likely than not have black friends. The elites fully support socialism and are gravely concerned with global warming, flying private from LA to Louisiana and Toronto to get tax breaks on their films, while paying effective tax rates on par with the national average. Then they justify it all by saying that the left has been right about every issue in their lifetime and they spend money to further the reach of the left.

The one flaw in that argument is that all the social policies done in the name of creating a more equitable society have achieved the inverse of their noble aims. Democrats have controlled virtually every major city in America for decades. The quality of life for the urban poor only gets worse. While I'm not into the idea of grouping people by race, this of course disproportionately affects African Americans and Hispanics. There are some clear culprits;

the social welfare system, neoliberalism, education, the prison industrial complex, single motherhood, the unspoken prejudice of low expectations, connected with the victim mentality actively and passively promoted by leftist values.

The Democrats continue to blame inherent racism in a country that had a black president for the last eight years and literally worships at the altar of Oprah, Michael Jordan, Beyoncé and Michelle Obama. They also blame systemic problems, but I am still waiting to hear a viable solution other than protesting racism and attacking real racists (Donald Sterling, Milo Yiannopoulos?), and people perceived to be racist (Charles Murray, Ben Shapiro, Steve Bannon), or Islamophobic (Bill Maher, Sam Harris, Steve Bannon, Milo Yiannopoulus, Christopher Hitchens, Ayaan Hirsi Ali), for not blindly accepting liberal policy as inarguable truth. Or worse yet, the witch hunt mentality that goes after any celebrity with a whiff of Trump support or "cultural appropriation" (whatever that means) in their Halloween costume.

As this class of liberal elites believes in mostly nothing but the enjoyable, ultimately hollow fulfillment of their material desires and acquisition of perceived power and control (I'm talking to you John Podesta and George Soros!), they replace religion with ideology, not unlike the Communist revolutionaries in Russia. Though they've convinced themselves that they are doing the right thing, for they are so open minded and tolerant, they are just blindly following the same patterns without questioning if their plans are making anything discernibly better. Since they are divorced from the middle of the country and reality, they don't even consider the implications of their welfare state, America's role in the foundation of ISIS and the radical Islamization of Europe.

Moderate elites don't even consider voting for Trump, because he's vulgar, he allegedly groped a girl on a plane in the 70s and bragged about how many hot girls he gets on the side to Billy Bush eight years ago in a private conversation. I've heard leftists claim Trump raped a thirteen-year-old girl, completely ignoring that Bill Clinton was accused of the same thing accompanied by the same person on the same "Orgy Island" no less. (I won't get into the accusations against him, because I generally like Bill Clinton and don't think people should be slandered without evidence.)

Then they cheer as their kids protest "fascism," wearing symbols of terrorism around their necks. If this were a fascist country, I think the students who tried to physically attack Charles Murray at Middlebury would have been suspended.

No one knows anything anymore and everyone is a hypocrite. Neither party has a viable solution on most issues, as party loyalty and populist dumbing down of politics to unimportant issues makes it so very little real change through politics is possible.

White is not black, it's green. Nothing makes sense anymore. Examining the divisions in these countries by policies and party lines is ultimately a futile exercise if we can't begin to bridge the gap by looking for commonalities. I saw the election of Trump as some kind of opportunity to reevaluate the parties and the broken political system. The post-truth world could be an opening to a revolution in our perception. If we could look at the opposing sides compassionately, even in spirited debate and consider the pros and cons of different perspectives honestly, we could awaken more fundamental truth. First we need to expose ourselves to uncomfortable truths by examining histories and facts before making a decision on an issue.

As it is now, the world is in decay, which is part of why mainstream

Democratic party positions now mirror extremist leftist values that consciously or unconsciously aim to destroy Western liberal culture. As Islamist leaders who studied political philosophy in America understood, individualism leads to nihilism. This is why half the country is willing to vote for something between a standup comedian and a conman, and half the country thinks American foreign policy is something on par with a sharia state.

I think America took the wrong lessons from history. While fascism is evil, building a society with shared values is usually not fascism. The selfishness of Ayn Rand that a lot of Silicon Valley types latched onto greatly damages society. Still, economic redistribution, though nice in theory will not fix inequality, because the world is not equal by nature. A desire for compassion and selflessness would be better. Something is broken on a much more existential level. We've created a world without meaning.

While critics of my argument would say Trump is using the Putin playbook, the left and right has being doing the same for decades. They just didn't have someone making a mockery of his office to make it so obvious.

While I think it is foolish to recreate the past like Trump's campaign suggested, I think it is valuable to investigate past errors, to see where we lost our way, in our plan to build something entirely new. People no longer even try.

Trump, like Obama, presented a desire to reform the country and though it was problematic, this is what pushed the forgotten majority to give the orange guy a chance. While his first hundred days haven't been earth shattering, aside from the public sentiment of anger and confusion, he could still do a lot of good. We should take example from Trump's optimism, as repulsive as he may be to your senses. Bickering and shouting will not solve anything. There needs to be a concerted effort to live within multiple perspectives.

With my ego, I am as guilty as everyone else and I want to overcome this nonsense. People have an inherent desire to connect and care for each other, but it's hidden deep inside the layers of hate, fear, fatigue and frustration. Our culture sends us these messages through sentimental entertainment, but our hearts feel something more selfish and sinister in the culture that we all unconsciously emulate. We seek easy comforts and pleasures to avoid looking at the powers operating us. These powers are the economies and the governments, but really these are our desires, which we don't really have any control over.

Though I've probably turned some of you off with my positions, I want to hear your suggestions for better alternatives. Maybe your suggestions will be the force that finds the meaning we've all been searching for. There will be a revolution in consciousness, and when the revolution comes it will depend on shared values that all of humanity, or some group that acts as an example for humanity wants and aims for. It might not be pleasant to face your self-interest at first, but the nihilism of both sides is in need of an antidote, and great things only tend to happen when there is a dire need for them.

We are social animals. We are also tribal animals, but breaking through disgust with different perspectives and tribes broadens our worldview. This is what is so troubling about the Social Justice Movement. Aside from it being boring to censor contrary or politically incorrect opinions and different kinds of people, it prevents growth and change, resigning us to maintain a level of distrust. This leads to more racism.

Unlike 1984, which is also happening with massive widespread surveillance, we self-monitor. We have become less free in the service of not offending one another. We're always castrating our behavior so as not to offend, even though this masks larger truths that have the potential to improve our current state of meekness and unhealthy resentment.

Society and individuals need pressures to develop and grow. Ayaan Hirsi Ali is always pivoting. Rather than victimize herself, she confronts the evil within the belief system that tortures millions of women. Still, she has an open mind. Branded an infidel by many, she still believes in the possibility of reforming Islam and has a desire to help those who are abused by faulty ideology. She sees it as possible, in spite of the horrors the men of faith showed her. Crazier things have happened.

If Americans could harness the power they hold together, they would shape the world far better than the elites currently driving the car. This depends on a willingness to compromise, because we live under the illusion that only by realizing our individual desires can we find our true selves, when in reality the best version of us lives when we lose ourselves in the thoughts, desires and concerns of others. This is where we create the space for love, the only force that can free us of the enslavement of our doomed personal and collective destiny.

On Politics

WHY ISRAEL IS DIFFERENT FROM THE OTHER NATIONS

As much as the world may have condemned Israel during its war with Hamas six months ago, the result of the state of trauma the nation faced was a good one. Israel was unified by a common threat. The feeling was visceral. Strangers consoled each other and looked out for each other's well-being, inviting even the homeless into bomb shelters as sirens sounded in the streets. While a small vocal majority was protesting the war, over ninety percent of the country stood united.

This unity was not directed against the foundation of an Arab state. It was a call to arms to protect a wounded nation that God had given mercy after the horrors of the Holocaust. People remembered what it meant to be Jewish, to stand as one man and one heart, while external forces tried to destroy them. As an American who had been living near Tel Aviv, it was shocking and emotionally disarming to understand what it meant to be a Jew. As the world outside fought over the merits of the war, it was clear to all in Israel that their existence was a miracle worth protecting.

Six weeks after the peace and order was maintained, the nation had one collective complaint. An anonymous post from an Israeli living in Berlin, revealed pudding cost four times as much in Israel as it does in Berlin. Adding insult to injury, the poster tagged the photo, "Olim L'Berlin," a phrase usually meant to describe one who makes "aliyah," the word that literally means ascendance, but is reserved for declaring one has escaped persecution to come to Israel. You can't make this stuff up. It was the most talked about topic in the country, as people contemplated defecting to Germany to combat the high cost of living and relatively low wages in Israel. A nation so close to realizing their mission to unite and work above their differences was now arguing over the prices of groceries and many people considered going back to the country where many of their parents and grandparents watched their families burn in gas chambers.

Bibi Netanyahu went from being savior of a sovereign state to a war criminal, and a country unified by a state of solidarity was once again split into thirteen parties that couldn't agree on anything. The elections will come on Tuesday and Israel has learned nothing. As seems to always be the case in the history of the Jewish people, they are united in times of suffering and feud with their egos in times of peace.

As Herzog, in his mild-mannered way campaigns on strengthening the middle class, repairing international relations and building peace with Palestine, Bibi will stand behind his impeccable national security, the romantic ideal of the Jewish State and the threat of Iran. The troubling aspect of this election is that it is not grounded on any clear reality. Nothing will change.

If elected, Herzog will stall a resolution with Palestine and not have the support of the government to make any of the domestic changes he campaigned on. Bibi, if elected, will continue to secure the Israeli borders and watch the economy grow by leaps and bounds, without significantly helping the common people.

Regardless of who takes the chair, Obama will reluctantly stand behind Israel, and Israelis will continue to complain about the cost of living, but be too petrified of the recent inferno of anti-Semitism to leave.

What is happening in Israel and around the world is much more sinister. People are being seized by apathy towards politics, because it is becoming clearer and clearer that no matter who is elected nothing meaningful will change in their lives. This is because the economy and political climate of the world is ruled by the human ego that only wants to receive pleasure for its own benefit. This is why Israelis contemplate exile into Germany over the price of cheaper pudding. It is always why Israelis can't agree on anything and we see two egos exploiting their own personal beliefs for less than 50% of the total votership, making alliances with ideological foes to secure a government.

The only good that will come out of this election is that the people will come to understand the old ways of doing things no longer work. Israel is not just another democracy lodged in the Middle East. It is in the Jewish DNA that their people must unite in order to survive the blows ahead of them and why the Star of David was lit when 50,000 gathered in Tel Aviv to protest Bibi, even when they were championing someone who naively claims we are in a position to make peace with a terrorist organization posing as a government. Israel is supposed to serve as an example for the rest of the world, but until we achieve meaningful unity in Israel, the name of the game is survival. As hatred of the Jews around the world continues to fester, the Jewish people will come to a point where they need to unite above their egos, but until that happens nothing will change.

TWO STATES: A MODERATE SOLUTION TO THE ISRAEL PALESTINE CONFLICT

As a liberal American Jew living in Israel, I am ashamed by the reactions of my peers to the election of Benjamin Netanyahu. The general sentiment of the majority of the Jews in America is that they are somehow superior to the Jews of Israel, who are racist, alarmist and treat the Arabs the way that Europeans treated the Jews before the Second World War. They clearly cannot reconcile how different they are from the Jews in Israel and how morally superior they are. Further, they cannot understand how the cheap theater of Netanyahu telling off Obama in Congress the day after praying at The Wailing Wall and tweeting "The right-wing government is in danger. Arab voters are going *en masse* to the polls. Left-wing NGOs are bringing them on buses," is rewarded with the election.

And the liberal Israelis are even worse. They see themselves as the sensible, elite minority that believes in a two-state solution, because they are the exclusive owners of compassion in a country full of backward religious fanatics. Somehow it is blind to most Israeli liberals that in reality most Israelis have the same relationship to faith as Europeans and Americans. It is shocking that the most educated and reasonable people in Israel by all metrics and conventions, the liberal elite, seem to have such a tenuous relationship with reality.

Their conception of a two-state solution in their minds seems to be drawn from listening to their parent's American protest albums. While Isaac Herzog, by all accounts seems to be a nice, convivial fellow, he is no Dr. Martin Luther King, and if he were elected, he would do exactly what the Gestapo, excuse me, I mean what Likud is doing right now. He would delay a two-state solution, that if he eventually found the correct terms to offer would be rejected, just as it was in 2000, 2001 and 2008, when Israel offered The Palestinians a state, with a capital in Jerusalem and offered fully cleared out Israeli settlements. What do these *Haaretz* writers expect will happen? Palestine will become a state and by some miracle it will become a bastion of civilized liberal ideals and not devolve into Syria. Did they forget that in March of 2002, terrorists killed 130 Israelis? Did they forget that the entire Middle East is a chaotic pool where terrorists breed and it may be dangerous to have such a country at your doorstep? Do they want to see Israel fall to the ground?

In spite of the shame I have for this American reaction, I can see why they are seized by confusion, unlike the Israelis living in Tel Aviv. While *Haaretz* and the mainstream American tries to paint a portrait of Netanyahu as a modern-day Mussolini, there is a clear dichotomy between what he says and does. Does he not at every opportunity try to improve the economic situation of Arab Israelis? The day after his election he said he supported a two-state solution, when we are able to draw up proper terms for such peace, which I believe is the reasonable way of looking at a country led by a terrorist organization that just lobbed thousands of missiles at Israel six months ago. While I believed the nationality bill to be a tad overblown, borderline totalitarian and racist, the realities that exist in this region necessitate the appearance of strength against a foe that will never, I repeat never, take anything that Israel offers them.

The only way Israel will come out of this situation is if Israelis find a way to compromise with each other. If a majority could recognize that there is a threat at our doorstep, we could find a moderate, left-leaning solution. Despite what American Jews believe, Bibi is a moderate, who only because of his belief he must protect Israel, panicked and banded together with the far right to get elected. The egos of the right and left are blinding us to our commonalities. A moderate, unified government and unified people in Israel is the only chance we have of coming to a tenable two-state solution with Palestine.

JEWISH AMERICAN EXILE

The lack of unity between Jews in the world today, to put it mildly, is concerning. The American Jews are particularly split, and these divisions of thought are only increasing. Formerly liberal Jews are moving further right in defiance of President Obama and others on the left wing are losing their allegiance with Israel, because of their desire for a two-state solution and general disgust with everything Benjamin Netanyahu says and does. Given the uncomfortable relationship that Israel currently holds with the rest of the world, it is not all that surprising that opinions about Israel are changing. It is also not surprising that J Street, a Jewish American liberal lobby group, supports Obama refusing to use its veto power in the UN to protect Israel.

Given that the election of Bibi Netanyahu has infuriated many Israeli and American liberals, it is inevitable that people will begin to stop supporting the Israeli state. It is also inevitable that supporters of Israel will become even more extreme in their defense of Israel. I know this as a fact, as a Liberal American Jew, living in Israel, whose head feels like it going to explode every time someone starts calling Israel an apartheid state. In full disclosure, it makes me want to champion everything Bibi Netanyahu says just to upset the contingent of American liberals who say Israel does not have a right to exist. The devil inside me wants to ask them to leave America and give the land back to the American Indians.

I think the problem with Israel is nothing more than its public relations. Israel's military has been so successful they are viewed as oppressors even though before the wall in Gaza was built, they were under attack on a daily basis. They are viewed as an apartheid state even though Arab Israelis live under full protection of the law. They are viewed as backwards and religious even though women and homosexuals are treated better in Israel than they are in the US. People ignore the fact that Jews were living in Israel before 1948 and no one wanted the land until Jews started to develop Jerusalem in the late 19th century. They don't seem to care that America was unwilling to give sanctuary to Jews before or after the Holocaust. It happened so long ago the history is lost on young American Jews.

Further with secularization and intermarriage constantly threatening American Jewish life there is a lot of ambiguity about what it means to be Jewish in America today. Most Jews go to temple three times a year, if at all. So how can someone define what it even means to be Jewish? It neither means to support Israel, or to be a liberal. Jewish food and humor have made their way into mainstream culture. Anti-Semitism clothed in anti-Israeli propaganda is starting to rise up on campuses, but not in a strong enough way to stir any unified reaction. So how can we ensure the survival of the American Jewish identity? And further, is it important?

In my humble opinion, the survival of the Jewish people around the world is nothing short of a miracle. Given the hatred of the Jews and the Holocaust, it is a miracle there is a Jewish state. The very values that liberals care for exist in Israel, but do not exist in the Palestinian territories, or even in the developed Arab world.

And even though the typical Jewish experience no longer involves being passed over for jobs because of a Jewish last name, anti-Semitism still exists and always seems to enliven throughout history when the Jews find sanctuary. The typical American Jew no longer exists. They are seemingly as diverse in thought and attitudes as America itself, but something about Jewish heritage is felt. This is because we as a people were once united and it lives in our collective memory.

Whether one denies their religion or practices with fervor, Jews feel connected by their heritage. If Jews do not have the ability to unite above these very real differences, there is a very real danger that the Jewish people will lose the heart of what it means to be Jewish, to be united as one man and one heart, as they received the Torah, the words that have kept the Jewish people together for thousands of years.

The Jewish DNA is liberal in nature, but it is important we care for ourselves before we care for the needs of people who don't believe we have a right to exist. When Jews are able to care for one another above their differences, in doing so, they care for the rest of the world. The only means for Palestine to be freed will come from the unity of the Jewish people around the world. The constant feuding between, religious and secular, Ashkenazi and Sephardic, conservative and liberal, will only work as fuel for the fire of anti-Semitism.

In order for the Jewish people to fulfill their role in the world, they must come to some sort of tacit agreement to protect their own interests. The Jewish people must not allow Obama to stop protecting Israel in the United Nations, which will always vote against Israel, no matter the issue, because of a voting bloc constituted in 1975 by all the anti-Israel Arab states and all the communist countries. As a neutral observer, it must seem a little odd that 40 percent of the UN Human Rights Resolutions were against Israel, even though genocide that makes the Israeli-Palestinian conflict look like a blip on the radar screen exists in many of the nations represented there. This is because there is not really a fair playing field in the UN, and the natural tendency of the world towards anti-Semitism will always blame the Jews for every problem that arises. While I am tempted to ask for more, all I want as a moderate, liberal-leaning Jewish American is for our people to do anything but aid in the destruction of the one place we all have sanctuary. Even Barack Obama, the enemy of the conservative Jews, is moderate enough for the time being to prevent this from happening, but if Jews continue to push the Democratic Party in this direction, it is frightening to think what will happen to Israel.

THE REAL REASON THE WORLD IS BOYCOTTING ISRAEL: IT HAS NOTHING TO DO WITH GAZA

A DIALOGUE BETWEEN JESSE BOGNER AND AARON CHESTER

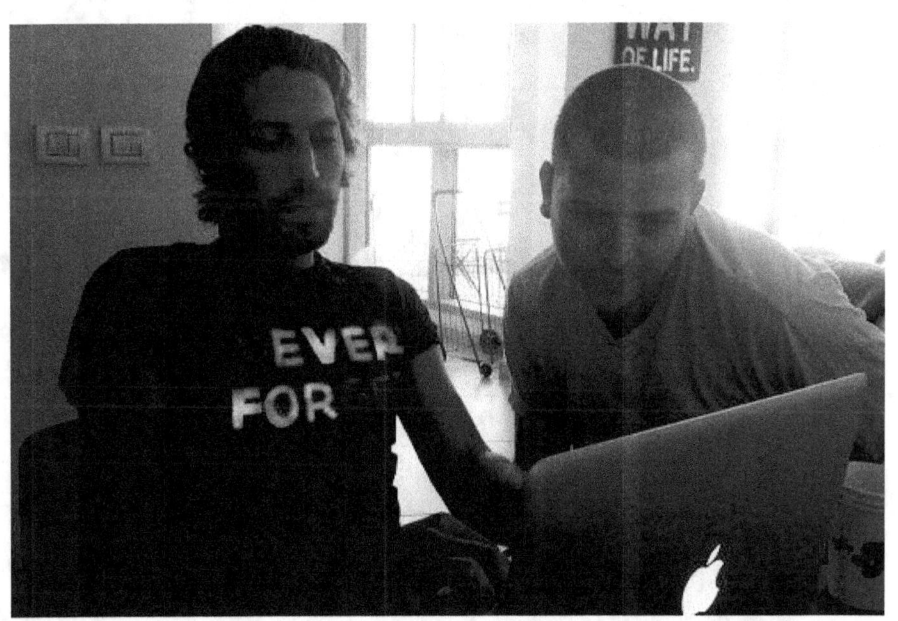

Jesse: Israel has gone from a nation that was almost universally seen as a bastion of peace and a story of triumph to the sole nation being blamed in the train wreck that is the Middle East. The recent boycotts and threats of boycotts of Israel products are part of a string of anti-Israel propaganda that has been developing for about a decade. The BDS movement has consistently been trying to marginalize Israel's right to exist under the guise of protesting Israeli occupation of the Palestinian territories. They do this by forcibly using their wide support net of both Muslims and liberals of all faiths, colors and creeds to pressure companies to boycott Israel for its occupation of the West Bank and Gaza.

This wide net of people as of late has included many Jews who would never openly call for the destruction of Israel, but feel a moral ambivalence towards the nation. Public opinion has made it not only fashionable to support boycotts of Israel, but liberal, normally right-minded people feel a moral obligation to put the disclaimer, "I don't support the occupation of the West Bank," to any positive musing about Israel. As someone living in Israel, I have to ask myself what is Israel doing wrong? This is because in my understanding of the situation, I never thought Israel was wrong to defend itself.

Some have argued Israel merely has a marketing problem and in all fairness Israelis in the media do not do themselves any favors. Unlike BDS and Hamas for that matter, Israel does not have a unified message that the public can cling onto. It certainly doesn't help when one of Israel's most respected journalists is saying in Haaretz that the boycotts are a light punishment for occupation and the Hadash party is signing off on the boycott.

However, I have mixed feelings about taking these people to task, because the fact that free speech, however deplorable is tolerated is one of the unique features of Israel in the region. This free speech does create a problem with public perception. If Israelis are symbolically in favor of Israel making itself vulnerable above securing itself from the wrath of terrorism and its enemies on all sides, what are American liberals supposed to think? If Israel is in the wrong it certainly makes sense for Orange to get out of its contract with Israel when it feels a clear financial benefit. Even the FIFA fiasco makes sense if the public perception is that Israel is a racist Imperial power that unnecessarily kills Palestinian children. The argument is extremely skewed when people forget that a decade ago suicide bombers were killing Israelis an average of 2-3 times a week.

I don't understand how this is lost in the argument. Just as I don't understand how people ignore that Israel was founded because most of the European Jews had been murdered in the Holocaust and the recent rise of anti-Semitism there clearly shows how unwanted the Jews are even today.

Aaron: And that's the whole point. The current boycotts and the anti-Israel movement in general is really not a rational one at all. On the normal political and socio-economic spectrum, it makes no sense at all that so much of the world feels negatively towards us. The boycotts and threats of FIFA, or Orange, or any other business, only show an escalation of a growing consensus that Israel is harming the world. And this escalation is a small one if we really think hard as to what could come next. The issue in fact is not political, or reasonable in any way, and that's why we need to go much deeper to get to the root of it.

You mentioned the Holocaust and its direct relationship with the existence of the state of Israel and how the world as a whole has as if forgotten this terrible atrocity. It's a real wonder, but then again it's a real wonder as to how this unimaginable horror happened to begin with and it is also quite unreal that the Jewish people, who had no interest in returning to what was at the time a desolate swampland, somehow ended up back in this tiny country smack dab in the Middle East. You would think we would be the good guys and underdogs in the eyes of the world, and that they would be praising the amazing progress we have made as a people after damn near complete annihilation, but we see this is not the case at all. Maybe there was a brief time when we returned to this land that the world saw us differently, but in general, we as Jews have never been viewed under the positive lens of the world that we are wishing for.

The nations of the world may think they are angry with us because of the Israel-Palestinian conflict, but this is not the case. As problems increase within every country's own borders, be it the U.S., or France, or anywhere else in the world, for some odd reason the focus on this tiny Jewish land in a sea of Arab Nations only becomes greater and greater. Today it is threats of cutting off business or sports ties, and tomorrow, who knows what? Today the reason is Palestinian occupation, and tomorrow who knows? The nations themselves are not to blame for their attitude to Israel, and they do not know why they are so preoccupied with this tiny dot on the map. Israelis also do not know why, and our boasting of our achievements and the Arabs' lack thereof do nothing for us, but cause more damage. But there are those who understand the whole picture very well, and they happen to be the very people that formed and maintained the nation of Israel for thousands of years. We survived many hardships far more difficult than boycotts, but we have forgotten how and for what reason they came to us.

The answer is quite simple. The nation of Israel is responsible for the happiness and wellbeing of the entire world. We hold in our hands the means to connect all of humanity, every nation and people, as a single harmonious family. Simply put, we are responsible for teaching the whole world how to "love thy neighbor as thyself." We as Jews and Israelis have forgotten it, and the entire world is actually not aware of it, but they so subconsciously feel that we are thorn that keeps digging deeper and deeper into this world.

Jesse: I feel like I might be boring the people who read all my articles, but there is a single solution to correct all these problems. Not only anti-Semitism, but hatred generally. Unfortunately, most people don't care to listen, but I feel compelled to shout it from the rooftops. I don't desire to blame anyone. All I want is for the world to understand that the force that prevents Israel and Palestine from connecting is the same ego that prevents neighbors and families for living peaceful happy lives. We need to invert our own desire into a desire to love others, feel their needs and care for them as we would ourselves. Whether you agree with this or not, you may feel incapable of achieving such a state. This is because our nature is to receive, to feel good. However, we find especially in Israel that self-seeking only creates misery. This is because Israel has a specific role it is not fulfilling.

Israel is not really a nation (we don't share geographical or racial commonality), but an ideological state that our ancestors agreed to. We only reveal God and the Torah by choosing to live as one man and one heart. If all the people of Israel demanded this state of our ancestors, these boycotts wouldn't be happening. These boycotts, rockets, and the rise of anti-Semitism are inevitable when Israel doesn't make the conscious choice to work above our nature to fulfill ourselves as individuals. Only with a force of love and unification will the irrational hatred of Israel disappear. All we need to do is connect with each other one person at a time until this reality will reveal itself. If we do not, eventually we will see we don't have any other choice.

UNITING A DIVIDED CITY: WHAT WE COULD LEARN FROM THE FALLOUT OF FREDDIE GRAY

A DIALOGUE BETWEEN JESSE BOGNER AND AARON CHESTER

This is dialogue between me and my friend, Aaron Chester, who grew up in the Baltimore area. Our goal was to find solutions to the tragedy that just occurred in his home town.

Aaron Chester: Having grown up and having lived the majority my life in the suburbs of Baltimore, and with the current climate of things across America, I can't say I'm all that shocked about what transpired as of late. Inner city Baltimore teeters on the brink of eruption every single day. There is such a divide in this city, drawn of course by racial and socio-economic lines, that when you put the right ingredients together—that you have in the death of Freddie Gray—, you end up with a true explosion. Of course, I see this from my own perspective, and I see that this is all madness.

I'm not living close by anymore, but I'm afraid for my family and friends that do, because what I see is young people who are angry and desperate, taking it out on society as a whole with violence, looting and destruction. I don't see it from the perspective of the inner-city African American kid, and I'm admittedly unable to. And they don't see it from any perspective other than their own either. And isn't this the problem in all of society after all? I say regardless of what happened to Freddie Gray, how could violence, stealing and destruction help anything? I see people destroying their own communities and hurting the people they claim they are fighting for. I don't say everyone or even the majority, but nonetheless there is a lot of that taking place. To me, Baltimore is a microcosm of cities across all of America, and we need to ask ourselves why is this taking place, how we solve it, and how each person in his limited view comes to sympathize and understand everyone else?

Jesse Bogner: The sad reality is that these riots happen all the time. It's nothing new and nothing really changes in these cities. It's very easy to see that America is split into camps, the haves and the have nots. Jon Stewart's coverage on how improperly CNN covered the riots expressed this perfectly. While Baltimore was set aflame in its frustration with a police force that killed a man in its custody, the elite of Washington was hobnobbing with celebrities. And what did

CNN cover? The red carpet for what twitter dubbed as "Nerd Prom," where Senators, news correspondents and TV actors cracked wise about Obama's administration. It very clearly expressed the huge divide between the elected officials' priorities and the disadvantaged, primarily black citizens of Baltimore, who after decades of oppression both mental and physical woke up and screamed, I just can't take it anymore. The fact that CNN chose to cover a self-congratulatory event is just a comedy of errors.

And while it would be convenient to paint this very clear picture of the urban poor and the elite, the problem in America is not so simple. There is the urban poor, who never are really given any opportunity to achieve the American dream, and are ignored until some cataclysm takes the center-stage before a return to relative normalcy, but there is also a segregation of people between all socio-economic levels. We live in a world where we all depend on one another, but in our personal lives, we care exclusively for those who are close to us. As long as we continue to be slaves to the current political structure, where lobbies led by millionaires and billionaires are the ones influencing political discourse, the needs of corporations and wealthy individuals will be addressed before the needs of the majority of Americans who live paycheck to paycheck. We are constantly told we come from a land of freedom, but this freedom does not exist in the country's current state. Do you see anything changing? Will we learn anything from Baltimore, or will it just be like what just happened in Ferguson last year?

Aaron: I hope we learn from this, and we have to. Now we see uncontrollable riots on a large scale in major metropolitan areas. We see that when angry protestors come together under one cause, whether it is to destroy or not, there's little that law enforcement can do to stop it. This situation must be looked at from both sides because failing to do so could mean widespread chaos and destruction throughout the whole country. If people are desperate enough to destroy their own communities, we have a real problem.

Jesse: While I understand Obama's take that this civil unrest is not solving any problems and the right wing calling card of guys like Matt Walsh who say that these riots "only deserve condemnation," what else is a voiceless population going to do? There is no course of action for the people of Baltimore to make any systemic change. However, by destroying their own communities these people are only hurting themselves. They will change the news cycle for a few days, but they are the ones who are forced to live in the aftermath of destruction.

Baltimore wisely has already arrested six suspects across racial and gender lines in the murder of Freddie Gray, calming the storm of frustration, but what happens next? What do you see as an alternative for this segment of the population with no hope? I believe that this progress must have some sort of benefit.

These people are coming to a point of frustration where they are going to have to look for alternative solutions. We can't keep things the way they are, where poor communities flare up in rage and return to the depression of normalcy and then flame up again. This cycle will not just continue. There has to be a breaking point.

Aaron: I'm not sure that we have come to this breaking point yet, but it is for sure a sign of things to come, and things can get much worse. In the end, I don't think the frustration is about racial issues or even socio-economic issues. These are the symptoms, but not the root of the illness. The root illness is the one that we all suffer from, in Baltimore, the U.S. as a whole, and throughout the entire world. This illness is the absence of connection between people and complete ignorance of how to live with one another in a proper way. Everyone needs to care for and sympathize with everyone else, from the government down to the common people.

We look at inner city Baltimore and we see the results of an education system that does not care for the people. The schools want to push their agenda while the youth go out to the street to a world that they have learned nothing about. Sadly, if there are no positive influences in the home environment, we come to a state of desperate, angry young people who are willing to destroy their own communities for the sake of being heard in some small way.

The equality that we dream about when we think of America is still just that, a dream. But we can change that. It starts not with the government, but with us, the common people. What can each individual do to begin to foster caring, loving relationships with everyone around him? One individual who begins to educate himself about how to correctly care for and relate to others will create a "trickle up" affect. We don't need to wait for something to "trickle down" from the government and the elites, because it won't happen.

Jesse: I agree with you that the solution needs to come from a fundamental shift in the way people think about and measure success. America was built on the foundation of the American Dream, the idea that everyone was entitled to a family, a comfortable life with a two-car garage and a lawn. We see that this dream is not a reality for a middle class that barely exists anymore. Our desire for more has not led to any kind of meaningful fulfilment. The pursuit of happiness has led to a culture of overmedicated, overworked, depressed people and left many populations on the fringes of mainstream American society with no hope for the future. Our egos lead us to believe happiness lies in material success and though some people are able to achieve this, it is necessarily at the expense of the whole society.

If we want the "hope and change" Obama ran his campaign on, we need to start looking at our communities holistically and learn that we are all connected and dependent upon one another. We need a method to create systemic change. The success of one individual will not benefit the whole, unless this individual is able to transcend his nature, which is to dominate and exploit people.

The way to achieve this change is through education. And not what we think of as education today. Adults and children need to learn that their success is dependent on the success of others. They need to see that coming to mutually beneficial solutions will lead to more success and greater happiness. Cooperation is what built this country. The general ego of the world makes pure capitalism, the way we see it today, works as a destructive force in society, where it used to create abundance. When profit is the only motivation in business, there is no concern about how corporations and banks affect people and there is absolutely no consideration for the future and sustained growth.

This force of the ego is why our once great cities and our most beautiful buildings have become copper mines for building the infrastructure of China. There is absolute lack of cooperation in Congress, killing any possibility of the government deciding on matters in favor of the majority, the way they were intended to, when the legislative branch was invented. All this chaos creates a framework of a frustrated population that will not accept the authority of a government that does not look out for their interests. Do you think there is a way that we can re-educate our population and our government to make decisions that benefit the entire country and ultimately the whole world?

Aaron: There is most definitely a way to fix things. Baltimore shows us that for better or worse, when people come together for some kind of cause, right or wrong, the government and the public in general must respond and change accordingly. I stand by the fact that destruction of any kind hurts those doing it and everyone else. I don't know what happened to Freddie Gray and how can I say I know how the inner-city population feels when I don't come from it? I can't, and herein lies the solution.

We need to conduct from the bottom up massive social reform from the people, where everyone has a voice to express to everyone else how he or she feels and why. It's not important whether or not we agree on solutions, what's important is what occurs when we all sit together from a place of true equality, for the sake of discovering a solution. Our government may be meant to create such solutions, but this solution comes not from a body of authorities, but instead from people coming together with each other. We need to build organizations in the community that will sit concerned people together with one another, workshops so to speak. In these workshops, we must educate one another about how to come to mutual understanding, connection, and care for each other, regardless of race, ethnicity, or economic situation.

Most importantly, through efforts made to connect and unite with the common goal of bettering society, we all truly come to empathize with one another. As nature has it, we are social beings that are totally shaped by our environment. The blame game is up because now it is each and every individual's responsibility to build a better future. We need each other to do that. Baltimore this past week exposed the symptom of a sickness that continues to spread. Yes, there is injustice in every realm of society, and yes we do not understand and care for one another in the way that is needed to live in peace. But now that the sickness has been revealed to some extent, we can begin with the remedy. The remedy is education, unity and connection. When we build this with one another, beginning with discussion groups and seminars in our own communities, the system will respond. We ourselves will change. Let's not let the suffering of all parties involved, especially the suffering of Freddie Gray and his family be in vain. The rebuilding starts right here, in the relationship between you and me.

Let us take a look at a few opinions of friends of mine living close to the situation and try and understand their thoughts without any judgment.

Sam Abrams (Baltimore City resident): This is not the solution and I don't think anyone thinks it is. This is just painful to watch. You're angry about poverty and injustice, but destroying your own community doesn't fix that. It sets you back 10 years. You could've had a march, and that would've been called for. This isn't even destruction this is a warzone. Racial divide needs to be fixed. I'm sure there's more brutality against blacks than whites but what does destruction accomplish? The biggest struggle now is who has to clean this up?

Michael Margolies (Baltimore City resident): Love is the answer! There is a tendency to try to find external "bad guys" who are to blame in nearly all situations. Instead of demonizing each other, let's humanize each other.

Brandon Havener (Serving in The National Guard in Baltimore): So far I've seen a lot more appreciation and peace from everybody. 98% of baltimore appreciates the guard for being here and protecting the city. Nothing violent at the harbor so far. There were protestors driving down the street honking their horns showing the peace sign. I think the majority of the protestors want a peaceful outcome.

Jesse: By expressing these kinds of feelings without judgment, we will be able to come to common solutions for a city that is plagued by destructive points of view that lead to destructive actions. Only by connecting and finding commonality will we be able to start making clear, achievable goals for a better Baltimore. If this city, with clear cultural differences and distinct differences of point of view, can come to connect, it will lead the entire country by example. Every bad situation is an opportunity to correct our thinking, allowing us to question the sadly unsustainable nature of American life.

THE LIGHT AT THE END OF THE TUNNEL

(Interview for TLV1 Radio at TedX White City, Tel Aviv)

The details of the last few weeks are horrifying, but expected. As stabbings take place all over Israel, not only in the terrorist hotbed of Jerusalem, the routine of the violence permeates through Israeli society almost like business as usual. People mention the stabbings casually, if at all. The security has increased ever so slightly in Tel Aviv and Petah Tikva (the sleepy Tel Aviv suburb where I live and study Kabbalah, where an Israeli man was just stabbed outside of a mall). The numbness is felt. There is little hope of ever solving this problem and the current government seems content to delay before doing anything substantial. I have yet to hear a convincing plan on how to move forward from any politician, but there seem to be distinct schools of thought.

There is the liberal perspective, the Shimon Peres perspective, that we should look at the source of this terror, find what the terror is the symptom of and the majority opinion of Israel that Netanyahu frankly declared to the Knesset this week, "We must understand once and for all, that terror does not come from frustration that there is no peace process. Terror comes from the desire to annihilate us (Israel)." Peres believes in a two-state solution, while I have yet to get a good sense of Netanyahu's thoughts on a solution, or even if he has a desire to solve the conflict.

My Father with Shimon Peres

Though my opinion is closer to the middle than Peres, it was refreshing to see him speak at the TEDx White City event in Tel Aviv. Somewhat surprisingly, it seems to me the person who sees the brightest future in the Middle East is the one with the least hope of being a part of it. At 92 years of age, Peres holds onto the ideals of his mentor, the hugely idealistic, somewhat macho first Prime Minister of Israel, David Ben Gurion. Peres described Ben Gurion as an "innocent man." His innocence was what made the foundation of Israel possible in Peres' mind. The same idealism was what I felt lurking in the halls of the Ted Talks. The exchange of ideas and a vision for the future is why Israel has evolved so rapidly, in spite of a dearth of natural resources and the constant threat of war and terror. This is why it has been so disheartening to experience the numbness of this last wave of terror. Unlike the war last year, people in Israel have not yet come together. There is no clear vision for the future.

However, I am hopeful. The darkness only appears to reveal the light at the end of the tunnel. As this terror grows more pervasive, it will force Israel to overcome together. We will have to, as Peres commanded and as the wisdom of Kabbalah prescribes, "forget the past," and look forward to create a new reality. Though I don't agree with Peres that the Arab world will reform itself with the self-education available to the young oppressed people carrying smartphones, I do believe the century of Zionism has made people too weary to try to create new solutions. The younger generation that has grown tired of politics needs to reform the corrupt system, by building something new out of the waste the older generation has left behind.

As Peres went on with his sage-like speech, I felt connected to his outlook, if not his policies. His seventy years of service to the nation of Israel made it clear that "ego is the smallest thing in life," and he offered a choice to the audience of thinkers "you can be either small or be great...if you want to be great serve other people, don't try to rule them." Big people, he claimed, served great causes above themselves and found solutions through the power of unity. As Israel is further burdened and tired of the same old violence, I am confident our consciousness will evolve and that peace will not be a utopian dream, but a real viable reality.

THE AMERICAN REVOLUTION HASN'T HAPPENED YET

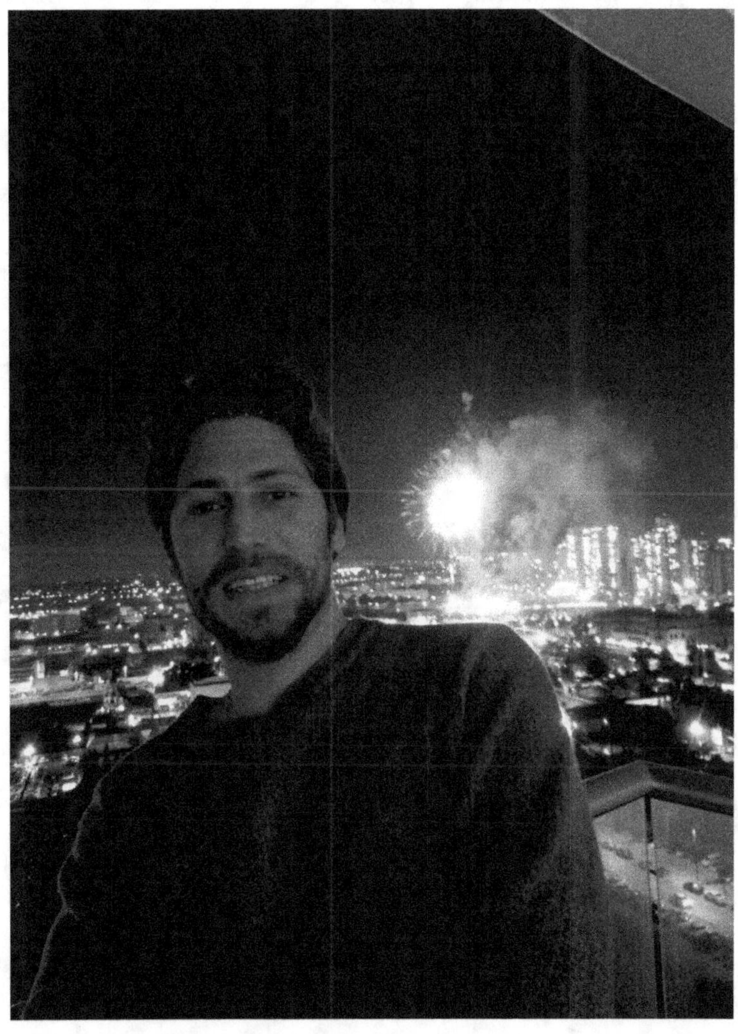

America has always associated happiness with the acquisition of wealth. When Thomas Jefferson wrote the declaration of independence, his original intention when he wrote "the pursuit of happiness," was to express the "pursuit of property." In the last few decades this pursuit of property has been unattainable for the majority of Americans as the gap between rich and poor increases exponentially. The American dream is failing. No longer can many young people realistically envision having more wealth than their parents.

Democracy and industrial capitalism closely mirror our instinctual egoistical desire to attain more without considering the benefit of the whole system. This is why the greatness of America in the mind of a patriotic person is the result of his or her ability to pursue individual prosperity and comfort. However, when this American dream becomes difficult or unrealistic to attain, what grows is an angry populace that has lost faith in the very systems that once brought its nation the greatest fortunes the world has ever seen.

This lack of faith is loudly expressed in the upcoming presidential elections, where candidates who appeal to the emotions of voters have captured the imaginations of the public. Donald Trump's slogan of "Make America Great Again," is appealing directly to this desire. He won the Republican nomination on a platform of xenophobia, the personal freedom to be politically incorrect and the need to run America like a business that wins negotiations with foreign powers and stops wasting money it doesn't have like a sieve. He is essentially trying to use the ego to recreate the past American system, a desire in the voters to return to a nostalgic version of America where great prosperity waits around the corner, which is patently impossible.

On the other side of the coin, Bernie Sanders wants to create a new economic model that curtails America's huge economic disparity and provides free college and single payer healthcare like Scandinavia. Though it would be near impossible for any of these promises to be fulfilled in a single presidential term when questions like, "Where will the money come from and how could these proposals pass without a huge congressional majority" loom, these revolutionary ideas are gaining widespread support from a population that has lost faith in its leaders. If in the most likely scenario, Hillary receives the democratic nomination it will not be because of her insider status and extensive experience, it will be because she can convince the country that she too wants to change the failing systems, that she is the only person who understands the process of making these changes and that the big banks donating money to her campaign won't affect her policy decisions.

What people fail to understand is that this desire to shake things up in American life comes from a spiritual lack that cannot be solved politically. When politicians and private individuals are all driven by their egoistical desires, greed will always persevere above the best interests of the majority. Even if Bernie Sanders were able to create a more socialist framework for American life, it would ultimately fail, because it would still be born out of a collective egoistical desire for free things, not a truly revolutionary shift in human consciousness. It would be recognition that it is too hard to attain personal wealth on one's own instead of a change in human desires. Socialism without a change in consciousness will never work, because it expressly goes against the ego, which strives to attain more to the detriment of others. The world needs to recognize that the force of the ego that is responsible for all of human development has become a cancerous cyst on humanity and nature.

We must recognize that our self-interest has created a world crisis in all spheres of existence, be it economic, environmental, educational, or social. Look at the rainforest and the polar ice caps and we can see the environment is literally destroying itself. These ecological phenomena all begin with humanity, the ego-driven dominant species of the planet that works in opposition to the system of nature where everything serves a purpose in the life of everything else, where everything works for the betterment of the entire world. The only choice we have is to redefine how we measure success in our world. We have to strive to repair our world over our individual desires and this is only possible if we make a decision to connect with each other specifically for this purpose. We need to care for the whole above even our own interests.

We need to shift humanity from egoists to altruists, but before we can achieve this we need to recognize our nature. Precisely because of our current egoistic nature we don't understand a single thing about reality. Like the politicians running for president, until we recognize the sickness of our ego and connect with each other to overcome it, we are only grasping at straws. Without a desire to work above our egos and a method to attain true connection, we will be unable to repair the world from its state of crisis.

At the **North American Kabbalah Convention** taking place this weekend in Newark, New Jersey (May 19th-22nd), one thousand fellow Kabbalah students will unite expressly for this purpose, as tens of thousands connect around the world on the internet around our common desire. From our humble beginnings, we believe we are taking a giant leap towards a revolution in human perception. By making great efforts to mirror nature and work above our egos, according to the wisdom of Kabbalah, we can create a new reality above the limits of our five senses. We will awaken a pure connection that can gradually serve as an example for the entire world. We will unconsciously influence the rest of the world. While we understand many people may find this pronouncement naïve, all great revolutions begin with naïve idealism. Was it not idealistic when a small group of Americans sat in a room and decided to pronounce themselves independent of the most powerful monarchy in the world on July 4th, 1776?

WHY DONALD TRUMP'S EGO WILL WIN THE PRESIDENCY, WHAT IT MEANS, WHY IT DOESN'T MATTER AND WHAT TO DO ABOUT IT

Having written a book about the collective ego of the world, entitled *The Egotist,* I researched the causes and consequences of the untamed ego and found a solution to the distress of the egoistic instincts that rule us. Given the openly egoistic nature of the first reality TV star turned presidential candidate, I can tell you our country is in for a heap of more trouble, not because of what he will do, but because of what this phenomenon represents. Though I would like to be cautiously optimistic that the most qualified candidate will win, I can almost guarantee—I feel it in my gut—that Donald Trump will be elected president.

As we saw in the early Brexit polls and later in the decision, people say they will vote one way until fear beats at them in the solitude and privacy of an election booth. Will this fundamentally topple American values? Probably not. There will be no wall to Mexico and no the Mexicans will not pay for it. In all likelihood Trump will return to the moderately conservative Hillary supporting values he had before he was trying to win an election with pseudo-fascist calls to take America back. The greater problem is what Trump spews seems to be what the people want.

Everywhere we look these days, the ego is driving people apart. Smart people, stupid people, rich people, poor people, black people, white people, Jewish, Chinese, short and tall people. To quote Depeche Mode, "People are people so why should it be, you and I should get along so awfully?" We can't seem to help ourselves. African Americans are fed up with the unfair treatment they have received from police and courts for generations, let alone the horrors of slavery that preceded the unfair treatment. Officers still fear for their lives working in crime-riddled communities. Mostly innocent Muslims are treated as enemies to the state, while everyone is communally afraid of the brewing Muslim extremism both in the United States and knocking at the borders.

There is an impending sense of hopelessness in all cross-sections of American life. Even the well-educated Upper Middle Class kid is graduating college with at least 100K of student loan debt. These conflicts and the failings of the system of American government are driving people apart, building anger and resentment that balloon the ego, both individually and collectively. While some may argue the hateful internet message board is the vilest place on earth, it is the nation's id and Donald Trump has succeeded in tapping into it.

In spite of this frightening proclamation, ego suppression is not a tenable solution. The ego is a delicate creature that cannot be tamed, and must be directed to a higher purpose. There is an alternative that has the potential to save humanity from destroying each other and the seemingly irreparable state of the planet we occupy. Since our nature is destructive—even self-destructive—

humanity is crying out to find a solution to the cycle of hatred that divides America and the rest of the world.

With or without religion, an angel and a devil guide people on either shoulder. The desire for the self usually works in opposition with the desire for a better world. As long as humanity is guided by self-interest, the ego will continue to grow destructively and the world will be plagued with irresolvable problems.

If we choose to see our troubles as an obstacle to overcome, a sign that it is always darkest before the dawn, we have a chance at connecting above our differences, in spite of the fact our leaders offer no solutions. In order to fix the problems that plague us, we as individuals must acknowledge that even though we know what is right, our ego will always be driven by our desires and our current environment that only feeds us the wrong desires. Our problems will not be solved economically or militarily, or with liberal pseudo-fascist decrees of political correctness.

Though we cannot change our desires we can change our intention to build a world where everyone has the chance to benefit if we decide to sit with one another and discuss openly what ails us. Instead of protests, our cities need to provide places where people can meet to discuss possible solutions to the crisis looming around us, with a structure where people agree to listen to each other and not interrupt each other, so they can learn to empathize with each other's feelings no matter how outlandish they believe them to be. By annulling the ego temporarily for this purpose, people will slowly learn to properly connect with and care for one another. My experience with the Arvut Social Movement in Israel and Connected Wisdom in America has convinced me that the workshop method is a clear pathway to better human connection that always works in spite of broad cultural differences. If the people demand better relationships and work for it, it will come and JFK's address of "Ask not what your country can do for you, ask what you can do for your country," will gradually replace the current American ethos of "this country is going straight to hell."

TED'S GREAT FOLLY

If Ted Cruz expected some sort of ovation for his non-endorsement of Trump last night he was gravely mistaken. This condescension and bravado is all based on this assumption by the Republican base—the strain of the party that champions its experience, moderation and fiscal conservatism—that Trump will lose the election in a landslide and that the Republican Party will have to recover from this sideshow that Trump put on 2020. The error of this reasoning, which seemed perfectly rational three months ago, is that Trump looks like he will not only challenge Hillary respectably, but he will probably win the presidency.

Like it or not Ted, but this is your party and they can't stand you. Further, if you go through the issues there is essentially no difference between the two candidates, besides the fact that Trump inspires disenfranchised white Republicans and Independents, while Ted Cruz only connects to the Christian right and creeps out just about everyone else. Yes, Donald Trump is in many ways a disgusting buffoon, but it's a little late to say he doesn't know what he's doing in this race and everyone who crosses him will be signing their own death warrant.

While Ted stands strong in his defiance of the party, all he did was further embolden the Trump supporters who couldn't stand him anyway. His fake outrage about things Trump said about his family only makes him look weak. The Republican Party has become the WWE, or more accurately The UFC—UFC President Dana White was actually a Day 3 RNC speaker who brilliantly compared his sport which was once compared to human cockfighting and is

now mainstream to Trump's rise in the election (God Help Us!)—
where people only respect strength. Politics have changed. No one
is impressed with Ted Cruz's old-timey rhetoric and Ivy League
snobbery. The Republican Party now follows people who speak
from their gut and put on a show.

If Day two was as the New York Times deemed a "low energy"
night, Day 3 was anything but. Ted Cruz, like a great wrestling
heel, in his defiance of a Trump awakened and riled up support for
Trump, without resorting to beating up on Hillary. It was a game
changing moment that unified rather than separated the party.
Cruz's dismissal will do nothing but help Trump in his race.

While Ted dominated the news cycle for 24 hours and made the
world forget Mike Pence exists, his idiotic belief that he was doing
the right thing and not saving his bruised ego was utterly tone
deaf. The decision to passive-aggressively condemn his own
party's nomination, a man who is wildly popular, may have killed
his political career. Why would anyone in his party trust him? Do
you really expect the Republican electorate who love Trump like a
family member will suddenly decide to go with the guy who tries
to sabotage Trump in 2020, in the event the man doesn't win?

TRUMP WILL WIN THE ELECTION BY USING THE INTERNET AS A TOOL OF OPPRESSION

A week ago the election was over. After strong showings in all three debates and the Billy Bush tape falling in Clinton's lap many polls showed Hillary winning by double digits. It was the sensible narrative that most smart people predicted all along. Trump would lose big and everything would be restored to normalcy. This would be like the Sarah Palin debacle, a footnote about this odd moment in American history, where one of the most patently ridiculous media stars in the world ran for president, and set the Republican party back for a decade. Shockingly, one of the most historically accurate polls conducted by the Washington Post and ABC News (you couldn't get more mainstream media) shows Trump is not only edging closer to Hillary, but he's actually winning the race by one or two points.

Nate Silver, the election guru who successfully predicted every state but one in the last two elections, looked very stupid predicting Trump could not win the primary without endorsements. Now his formula is giving Trump a 29% chance, up from 9% a few weeks ago. The weakness of Silver's analytics method in such an unconventional race is that it fails to factor in what happened when Brexit passed. Trump supporters like Brexit supporters are much more passionate than liberals (many of whom can barely stomach Hillary and wanted someone who represented real change like Bernie). The right will be getting to the polls with fervor and uniting together to make sure they get to election booths. They will also get the closeted socially conservative voters who secretly want the wall to Mexico, are fed up with Caitlyn Jenner and don't see the point of letting in 55,000 Syrian refugees, which Trump has repeatedly unsubstantiatedly said could be anywhere from 200,000 to 650 million. This is why as I predicted in July and repeated on my Facebook page two weeks ago when people thought I was crazy, Trump would win.

Half the country is absolutely perplexed how this is happening. How can a pussy-grabbing narcissist with a penchant for lying pathologically be winning the presidential race? While it's spoken about like one of the great mysteries of our day, it's actually very easy to see how Trump does nothing but win. Like Bernie Sanders convinced half of the democratic party, Trump has made the argument that the corporations and banks that support Hillary are destroying America and that the mainstream media is owned and operated by these corporations.

The fact corporations and banks do horrible things routinely, with the built-in protecting the shareholders excuse, does make these conspiracy theories all too plausible to hundreds of millions of Americans. He also repeatedly calls Hillary "Crooked Hillary," to reinforce this point so much that even generally liberal uninformed voters believe Hillary is more corrupt or prone to lie than an average politician, when by the standards of a run of the mill tea party candidate or Donald Trump she's Honest Abe Lincoln.

It isn't hard to ask one's self how this came to be. What elevated obvious con artist tactics to the presidential stage? The problem begins with a population that is willfully misinformed. Out of the dust of Watergate, Paddy Chayefsky's vision of a decaying world, the 1976 film *Network*, alerted us to the dangers of the propaganda machine called television. The film brilliantly illustrates how profit margins and ratings were killing the once pure (at least not driven by profit) news divisions of television networks. It was clear the viewers raised on the tube didn't have the attention span or the desire to keep informed. They craved spectacle, and thus they glued themselves to Howard Beale, a mentally unstable "truth-teller," screaming about the injustices of the world. This ratings bonanza lasted up until Beale began to get to the true crux of the truth, which was that nations, ideologies and individuality were all lies in the service of global banking system that operates everything. The message was too depressing. Beale lost his viewers and to salvage the network the executives planned his execution, which would take place on live television. While the film is highly nuanced and doesn't aim to illustrate a single point, what stuck with me is that most people aren't driven by rational thoughts and figures, but their emotions. They don't want to confront reality head on. When Beale convinced the people to express their anger to be an instrument of change, he gripped them, but when he told them the truth that no matter what they did nothing would change, he was destroyed.

Today *Network* almost feels quaint. Not only is all television news done in the Howard Beale mode of commentators expressing fake outrage and distracting us from real issues, but hard news is dying and being replaced by the internet. Newspapers don't have the budgets to cover local politics, which will almost certainly lead to unprecedented corruption. Politicians have been lying to us probably since the beginning of time, but there were once checks and balances. There was this assumption that if politicians lied, the press had the responsibility to confront the liar and find the truth. The internet's vortex of irrational conclusions and conspiracies, along with Trump's dismissal of the media, has made the media irrelevant, and the noble intentions of the originators of the internet to share information has been disproven. The internet became a device to watch porn, listen to music and share misinformation.

In the 90s, many charlatans and geniuses alike had grand utopian ideas about the positive consequences of information sharing on a new consumer product called the internet. They sold a lot of Wired Magazines with druggy youthful optimism that information could set us free from tyranny. There would be a truly democratic space for the expansion of thought and exchange of ideas and true equality. While the evolution of the internet has been fascinating, neither wholly good nor bad, it clearly falls short of the noble hopes early adopters had for the information superhighway. It is a purely democratic space, where everyone has the freedom to innovate and share innovations. The problem is that it does exactly what people want and gets much better at this as it evolves. Much like democracy, it is a fair but not necessarily moral system, and as it gets smarter it gets to know what we like, making us more complacent and splintered into subcultures and unaware of the thoughts and groups we disagree with. It divides and weakens us by feeding us exactly what we want. And we frankly don't want to know the truth.

It doesn't matter that Trump's statements are mostly false to bald-faced lies 70% of the time to Hillary's 25%, his confidence and tendency to say politically incorrect things without an ounce of apology projects honesty, while Clinton's political expertise and lack of perceived sincerity paints her as a corrupt liar. Facts no longer matter to the majority of voters. It doesn't matter that the economy has grown by leaps and bounds in the last two years, when Trump describes the wasteland of Chicago as he claims Mexico is laughing at us. Trump understands better than anyone that people no longer pick candidates based on reason. Statistics don't matter. People vote in numbers, when they are swayed into the booths by their emotions.

This is why Barack Obama was able to destroy the seemingly clear incumbent Hillary in 2008. He extolled hope and change, while Clinton tried to deflate the optimistic message in favor of something more realistic. Hillary knew how government worked, which is something Obama needed to discover in his first term. As Obama described on Marc Maron's podcast WTF last year, the job of the president is to make slow change:

"Sometimes the task of government is to make incremental improvements or try to steer the ocean liner two degrees north or south, so that ten years from now, suddenly we are in a very different place than we were at the time. But at the moment, people may feel like we need a 50-degree turn, we don't need a 2-degree turn. And you say to yourself, well if I turn 50 degrees the whole ship turns 50 degrees and you can't turn 50 degrees.

It's not just because of corporate lobbies. It's not because of big money. It's because societies don't turn 50 degrees. Democracies certainly don't turn 50 degrees and that's been true on issues of race, issues of the environment, issues of discrimination. As long as we are turning in the right direction and making progress government is working the way it's supposed to."

Hillary is promising this form of practical incremental change, and it isn't sexy. Trump is taking his lessons from Obama's first campaign to promise the world. This is the meaning of "Make

America Great Again." No matter how impractical his plans and lack of plans are, his supporters and many people from both sides are looking at the recent wave of terror and a country divided by racial lines, and feel the need for a 50-degree change Hillary fails to promise.

The sensationalized media on the right does paint a picture of America that is broken and irreparable. The figures do the exact opposite. By invalidating the last vestiges of responsible media and the facts and statistics they trade in, Trump has been able to paint whatever picture of America he chooses. Scarier still, the rallying cry of Trump supporters that Americans are brainwashed by the mainstream liberal media has them disseminating the conspiracy-theory ridden far right diatribes of sites posing as legitimate news sources like Breitbart and The Blaze, as well as straight-up conspiracy theory sites making the misinformed views of crazies not as valid, but more valid than the mainstream media they claim that Hillary controls and the corporations use to brainwash the public so that America's elite can maintain their power. It doesn't matter that Trump plans to cut taxes for these evil corporations from 35% to 15%, because Trump is immune to rational attacks.

An uninformed and misinformed population sees reason as an enemy to progress. The tyranny of the majority that Alexis de Tocqueville predicted in his study of *Democracy in America* in 1835 is becoming a reality, wherein he found that "Social frustration increases as social conditions improve." A majority of voters, with little to complain about as evidenced by the median income of a Trump supporter being above the national average at 70k a year, want to subvert the rights of Mexicans, the LGBT community and Islam, to regain a country they feel they are losing hold of. While there are people expressly advocating hate speech since Trump has lifted the bar on the admittedly overly sacrosanct political correctness of liberals, the majority of Trump's minions I see posting on the internet take cues from their hero attacking Hillary relentlessly. Without a good BS detector, by looking at the comments on my Facebook page it would be clear that Bill Clinton is a serial rapist and child molester, and Hillary has devoted her life to covering this up.

Hillary wants to bring millions of refugees without knowing who they are and where they come from. Hillary orchestrated the Iran Deal (though it was enacted years after she resigned as Secretary of State) in order to ensure a nuclear bomb will destroy Israel. She knowingly funded ISIS and beyond that, murdered many rivals over the course of her long political career, to hide this, as well as to cover up the bribes she gave and investments she made. While a rational person knows these claims aren't remotely true, there is enough misinformation packaged convincingly enough to prove to many people that Hillary is the devil incarnate. In an investigation last week, The New York Times spent time with Trump supporters so stuck in their bubble that they believe if Trump loses, it means the election is rigged and many were weighing the pros and cons of toting their guns and starting a second Revolutionary War. Hillary, win or lose, should be very afraid for her life.

The distrust for institutions that began after the JFK assassination and were confirmed under Nixon, reached a boiling point in 2008, when Wall Street awarded bonuses to many of the men and women who collapsed to the economy. By 2015, the film adaptation of Michael Lewis' *The Big Short* was a hit and the time to process how hard things were a few years ago in America, made people rightly lose faith in institutions. People seem to forget the idiocy of Ted Cruz filibustering to shut down the Federal Government. This total lack of faith in systems made it possible for Bernie Sanders to nearly win the Democratic nomination by chastising Hillary Clinton for things like her friendship with Lloyd Blankfein, the CEO of Goldman Sachs that many people think should be behind bars. Even though Sanders didn't have a clear plan to reform Wall Street, his desire to spoke to people. While unlike Sanders, Clinton is a politician that weighs corporate interests to ensure her political power, something tells me that she didn't wait this long to ascend into the throne of the presidency to let Lloyd Blankfein make decisions for her. Though she is a moderate candidate in most respects who has done some things you probably disagree with, she takes the responsibility of the presidency seriously. She wants to make incremental changes in government that improve the quality of life for the majority of Americans. A safe, tough, and experienced candidate who has always been relatively conservative is not going to destroy the foundations of America.

The fact Hillary takes meetings with some truly terrifying world leaders who donate millions of dollars to her foundation is not the same as an irrational and unstable man who wants to tear Mexican families apart and build a gigantic wall, create a tariff and tax system that will destroy the American economy and knowingly denies doing and saying things he does on CNN like mocking a disabled reporter.

Trump has no respect for the truth, uses the legal system to stiff people he owes money to and threatens people who criticize him publicly, while creating personal vendettas with anyone who ever dares criticize him. Are these really the traits of an effective leader who will often be weighing two bad options? Like all politicians who make tough choices, Hillary's record is not spotless. However, Hillary's ties to strange bedfellows are a necessity in our complex global world, not evidence that her and Huma Abedin are puppets of the Muslim Brotherhood. As clear as this is to you and me, I urge you to read the mire being spread by your friends and family to do your best to change one vote calmly and rationally, because this election is going to be a nail-biter.

ONE LAST PLEA FOR HILLARY CLINTON FROM A LIBERAL WITH MANY CONSERVATIVE LEANINGS

WARNING: SOME OPINIONS HAVE CHANGED A LOT DUE TO THE POST-TRUMP LIBERAL HYSTERIA I'VE WITNESSED

Last week I wrote an article on how Trump is manipulating the public by convincing them the media is lying to them. What this allows Trump to do is make outrageous claims that have no bearing in reality. Then the Internet becomes this hazy place where assertions devoid of evidence and conspiracy theories convince relatively smart people that Trump is honest and cares about the middle class, while Hillary is some sort of Illuminati elite who purposely destabilizes the Middle East for personal gain.

On my Facebook page this point was proven with a flurry of negative, though about half positive responses. Some of my favorites are "FUN watching lamestream media desperately try to spin. #SpiritCooking. Next they'll spin Chelseas inverted cross. (She wants to be evil just like Mommy)," as if I, as a blogger who has never been employed by the media, am a lamestream media consultant. Others that I found clever from my adversaries were, "Lol what misinformation are you referring to exactly? The entire Democratic Party is just a organized crime cartel that trump wants to lock up! GO TRUMP!" My mother who disagrees with me, but is proud of me for sharing my opinion, cheering on Trump with the rallying cry, "Drain the swamp!" and another stranger let on, "You can't fix stupid." Since my work seems to be a bitter source of division, I want to make very clear where I stand on this issue, especially since I have had to go against the grain of my spiritual teacher, who I believe is the wisest man in the world. Also in retrospect, I think it was a bit long and rambling.

There are very clear reasons not to support Hillary Clinton. She, like Obama, George Bush 1 and 2, Reagan, Clinton and for all I know all of the presidents who were in power before I was born, is an establishment candidate. As a politician who depends on the financial support of corporations that include big banks, the military industrial complex, morally reprehensible lobbies (from things like oil companies, Monsanto, cigarette companies, gun activists) and the drug companies that gauge the American people, making Obamacare in the words of Trump, an absolute disaster. This is where the pay for play scandal comes in. She also has no respect for privacy, has not mentioned Guantanamo and very much like Obama treats whistleblowers that I believe are advocates of free speech like traitors to America. On the other hand, Trump called for Snowden's execution, before seeming to have no problem with whistleblowers when they try and swing the election in his favor.

Though on most social issues I am very liberal, there are things I am to the right of the Pope on (I never expected Francis would make that phrase irrelevant). I do not think it is smart to bring in Syrian refugees with the exception of women, children and the elderly. I am disgusted by the neo-liberal calling card of political correctness and forced multiculturalism that has made the generation a few years younger than mine weak, entitled and more interested in culture that promotes safe ideology than asks pressing questions and values artistic merit, that like fascism create witch-hunts when people express contrarian opinions. I also believe the media and our school curriculums promote this politically correct group think ideology that limits free thought, tries to convince us there is no biological difference between men and women and that Israel is more oppressive than the radical strain of Muslim ideology that has infected at least 100 million people.

In spite of this, I not only respect Hillary, but believe she will be the candidate who fights for the people that support Trump, the struggling middle class that has been conned into thinking trade tariffs, lowered taxes for the rich, lowered taxes and less regulations for corporations will improve the economy and income inequality. Her decisions within the admittedly corrupt system are done in the interest of the majority of Americans, not just corporations and the top 1%. Trump's economic plan to lift restrictions and lower taxes for the very rich and corporations is something that Republicans have claimed will help everyone for 40 years, but has proven to do the exact opposite.

I will lay off my disgust for his misrepresentation of truth and blatant disregard for everyone but himself and the people who advocate for him. Still, I would like to remind you that he will be appointing two, likely three or four supreme court justices who could very well repeal Roe v. Wade, marriage equality, continue the repealed limit on individual donations to campaigns (the catalyst of corporations running Washington). Thankfully (if Hillary is elected), a liberal court has a good chance of limiting the proliferation of guns people have no business owning, repealing the death penalty and ensuring transgender people are afforded the same rights as other citizens.

Another topic many people brought up in my circles is Israel. As a supporter of Israel, who has lived there for over three years, I have no reservations voting for Clinton. She has explained time and again, her nuanced position on the subject. Unlike Obama who seems to be working from the point of view that Israel is acting in violation of international law, in spite of the fact the settlements in Israel are necessary for Israeli security. Israel's other supposed violation of international law of bombing populated areas I believe is invalidated by the fact that Hamas fires from populated areas and warns the Palestinian citizens before these areas are hit. Never mind the fact that Israel goes above and beyond to fly the wounded to first rate hospitals and treat them free of charge, as well as provide free electricity and running water to their enemies during wartime. The biggest voices in Israeli politics with the exception of the fanatically right-winged Naftali Bennett (Netanyahu, Herzog, Livni, Liberman, the deceased Peres) all have tremendous respect for her.

In spite of my teacher's belief that Clinton will continue Obama's policies in Israel, I don't buy it. Just as I disagreed with him on Brexit, which the UK is fighting for their life to overturn (because of irreparable economic devastation), I disagree that Trump is the man capable of disempowering the political establishment.

If you don't care about America doing well and want Trump to get elected so he will put America in a crisis mode that will require new solutions from both parties, I think that is a reasonable reason to vote for Trump, which is the point of view of Slavoj Žižek and Julian Assange, both of whom I have tremendous respect for. I don't think it will work, but I understand the logic. I'm just sickened by all the lies and misrepresentations Trump is manipulating people with. If you think Trump is going to help the middle class, defeat ISIS quickly, resolve the crises in Syria and Libya (problems admittedly Saudis that have a good relationship with Hillary helped instigate) and solve problems of division in America, you will be disappointed. However, it's fine if we disagree.

I don't think politics will ever solve the inherent problems in the world, which are the result of our egoism. Trump is not to blame for this. We are. If the American public had any interest in staying informed and making rational choices, the probable scenario of a Trump presidency would not be staring at us in the face. Just to make the crux of my argument clear, I will put it here in **bold. Hillary Clinton is not a saint. She has participated in a corrupt system in a Machiavellian way, but the reasoning for this beyond just a thirst for power. It is to make life better for those who suffer and the majority of Americans. Sometimes this forces her to make decisions that are difficult to justify and sometimes she is wrong, but unlike Trump who virtually all experts predict will cause chaos if his policies are enacted, she is a stabilizing force.**

WILL TRUMP WAKE AMERICA UP?

The post-Nixon era was increasingly distrustful of authority and paranoid, in an increasingly global world with a cast of shady characters playing a major role in international policies and finance. The Reagan Administration, like Nixon and Kissinger, understood this shift in geopolitics. The role of the president was to simplify these problems regardless of the truth. The world became more global and interdependent. Saudi oil and The Red Scare had forced the United States to make strange bedfellows in the Arab world and the East. The best way to deal with countries that did not share democratic values in the Middle East was to divide, to push Sunnis and Shias against each other to take their sights off the West and prevent one nation from asserting its dominance and becoming a superpower. In order to distract Americans from uncomfortable truths and imminent threats, The Reagan Administration told a series of lies that made logical sense.

One example was the myth of Gaddafi. Though Libya was insolvent, marginal, and powerless, Reagan convinced the media that Gaddafi was a real threat to America as an excuse to avoid going after Iran and Syria, who actually killed American citizens with suicide bombers. You may remember he was killed in 2011 by a US predator drone.

The Obama administration continued this strategy of division of foreign powers and misdirection of American public opinion, in regards to conflicts in the Arab world. After Obama ran as an anti-war president, we are still fighting in Iraq and Afghanistan, after having sold 90 billion dollars in weapons to Saudi Arabia who funded ISIS and brokered a deal to pay their mortal enemy Iran 150 billion dollars over ten years, ensuring the Syria conflict, which Obama started with his inaction after vocalizing support for the Arab Spring (excepting Libya), will be a proxy war that will go on in perpetuity. The left remained silent, just as they did when Obama gave bonuses to those who created the financial crisis, instead of jailing them for their gross negligence and fraud. Though Obama made some nice social reform at home, his flawed policies were hidden to the majority of people who were too busy or self-absorbed to care. The actual world looks like a conspiracy theory.

While many believe that Trump is just plain dumb, racist, in above his head and lucky, he won the election with the cards stacked against him by making his own rules. When the picture mainstream politicians present is contrary to reality and the objectivity of news is compromised by party lines and fear mongering, Trump understood that facts no longer matter. When the left expressed their outrage, mostly on social media, they did so mostly to like-minded people. 90% of the country votes for their party no matter what and the 10% that chooses the election tends to be somewhere in between open-minded and batshit crazy. Though there were some sane conservatives who refused to vote for Trump, this wasn't a major factor as many liberals had predicted. Trump tapped into the rage and paranoia of the dying middle class, meshing conspiracy and fact together in his attacks of both his overmatched Republican competitors and Hillary Clinton. It was more important to be provocative than precise, as fake news and WikiLeaks swung the election for him on social media.

The fact that fake news in the three months leading to the election had more exposure than real news on social media, is just one form of confusion Trump used to catapult himself into the nation's highest office. It's hard to think of a single policy he didn't flip flop on. His public display of inconsistency was something America had never seen before. He sounded almost like an occupy Wall Street protestor one day and gave KKK speaking points the next. To many "Make America Great Again," sounded a hell of a lot like make America white again.

He built distractions in the form of common enemies for his base to rally against however their hearts desired, often in the form of pure, unadulterated bigotry. He put targets on the back of elites, "Mexicans sending drugs and rapists," all Muslims, low energy Jeb, little Marco, Ted Cruz's father and his role in the JFK assassination, indirectly "the blacks" mostly by proxy of Obama, Wall Street, Sidney Blumenthal, Huma Abedin, Iran, campaign contributions, China, ISIS, Big Pharma, Crooked Killary, "fake news" like CNN and The Wall Street Journal, and countless others, that he lumps together effortlessly, completely absent of logic, painting a picture of corruption in all elements of politics and society. He presents an air of authenticity that he too sympathizes with your plight, and since he never hesitates to tell you, "I'm really rich," or "I'm really smart," people assume he knows something they don't and he has the wherewithal to fix it. If he were a conventional candidate, in say 2004 when Howard Dean lost the nomination for yelling excitedly, scandals would have forfeited his candidacy maybe a dozen times. In spite of all this, I'm not any more concerned than I was last year, as someone who ideologically agrees with Obama on virtually every domestic issue.

The millennials are asleep. The older generations have been sleeping at the wheel for decades. As the world's problems become greater and more nuanced than the average person has the time or desire to delve into, somewhat distrustful of politicians, we still cling to the hope that these political candidates have our best interests at heart. It's true that many of them may, but all politicians are aware that the promises they make are largely empty ones. Since we live in a world where politics is really a game of distorting uncomfortable truths and we have our own lives to deal with along with much more desirable entertainment and leisure opportunities regardless of our earning power, many of us have this fundamental belief that there are still real differences between political parties' other than the fact they seem to vote together no matter what in Congress.

In reality, other than what they profess to do in their campaign speeches, politicians are largely the same, because they are not working for the people directly. What politicians say and what politicians do are not remotely compatible. These speeches where Obama professed American values and his own largely sensible values are theater. A commissioner of a sports league claims to represent the players, really just balancing the demands of the player's unions in a way that ultimately best serves the billionaire team owners. A president protects the interests of the people, in a way that is geared towards the interests of banking institutions and large corporations who really dictate American policies. If it weren't clear that self-interest is the prevailing truth of Wall Street and all ruling powers, it would be an easier pill to swallow.

This lifting of restrictions, now popularly dubbed as neoliberalism, worked reasonably well for much of the 80s and 90s until about the year 2000. While Reagan tax cuts for the rich under the umbrella of trickle-down economics threatened this upward trajectory of mass consumption culture, the internet boom of the 1990s allowed Americans to bask in their nation's immense wealth for the time being. This is no longer the case. The gap between rich and poor is edging closer to the pre-depression robber baron days. 0.1%, what Bernie Sanders would call one tenth of one percent of the population owns as much as the bottom 90%, while the 62 richest people in the world own as much money as half the world's population. This begs the question how did this happen?

Following a swath of policies that cut restrictions in order to stimulate growth in a nation carrying a huge budget deficit, Bill Clinton's economy was kicking ass with fiscal conservatism and the opportune development of the internet. He cut spending, closed the deficit and let Wall Street run the economy, with computer systems that supposedly could hedge bets to make sure the economy could sustain itself even in states of catastrophe. When Glass-Steagall was overturned in 1999, banks were given the freedom to merge together commercial and investment banking, limitlessly trading derivatives and options that caused the financial crisis. Mortgage-backed securities (MBSs) and collateralized debt obligations (CDOs) were a loophole which allowed investment banks to buy loans bundled together as a single asset, a bond. These bonds, which the ratings institutions were pressured to mark as low-risk when they were anything but as they contained sub-prime mortgages, automatically inflated the value of the banking institutions. Additionally, there were derivatives, which were essentially gambles on mortgage-backed securities and CDOs. In order for the capital to keep flowing, these institutions encouraged lenders (sometimes shady ones) to keep giving mortgages and loans which had virtually no chance of being repaid. This worked until so many people were foreclosed on that the CDOs and MBSs lost their entire value and the banking system was on the brink of collapse. Essentially, the banking system's success was based on a lie, that only favored the elites and nothing substantial has changed.

Though the economy is in much better shape than when Obama entered office months after the financial crisis, the majority of the people didn't see much of a recovery. When Hillary Clinton, the wife of the president who decided against government spending in favor of placing the reins of the government in the hands Ayn Rand's dear friend Alan Greenspan, is proclaiming the banking system is stacked against us, it's not difficult for Trump to present himself as a confusing stack of contradictions that wants to fix blatant injustice and bring jobs back. Never mind that by all indications Trump's plan to lift banking restrictions and further neoliberalism is not going to change anything. It's already happening. Of course, "the wall" is a terrible monument to racism that I don't believe will get very far and it is somewhat likely Roe v. Wade will be reversed, but there may be a silver lining to the brash man who stirs so much vitriol.

If people continue to protest Trump's bogus appointments and decrees, unite in the face of a clearly broken system, Trump may be held accountable for the poor job he is likely to do. Maybe our self-centered culture will be forced to fight for what is right, instead of sitting home in front of our computers blind to the state of disrepair our nation is creating. Income inequality wasn't always the rule of thumb. FDR fixed injustice, by creating banking restrictions and the establishment of labor unions (that of course also became largely corrupt), which protected workers' rights and protected banks and large corporations from themselves. In an economically stable 1960s, the young generation turned their attention to social injustice. The civil rights movement and the women's rights movement played a large role in creating a more equal playing field. When those rights start to be taken away, the younger generation of Americans may have the motivation to change the world once again. Those in power might be held accountable for the faulty system of government we let hurt us and damage the balance of the world for far too long. Maybe the protestors and other concerned Americans will be able to do what Trump claims to want to do by "draining the swamp," and create a society where the best interests of the majority are taken into account. An informed populous is a weapon that the Americans have willfully given up. Let's take it back and build a country with new values.

(Nothing of the sort happened)

THE RESPONSIBLE THING TO DO

(Source: Wikipedia Commons)

Aside from Lena Dunham leaving the country, it's hard to see any upside in this. Watching what seemed like an inevitable path to Trump's victory, I ran the gamut of every conceivable emotion, as you can see on my personal Facebook page, where I interacted with more people online than I had all year. I predicted this six months ago and in a fury warned every person in my mailing list a week ago (in a desperate email full of broken links and typos), feeling like it was my responsibility to show people precisely how Donald Trump was lying to them and begging them to do all they could to get Hillary Clinton elected. In these articles, I outlined why Trump would win the election, as I predicted in July and why it was important to stop him. In spite of my detest for the liberal politically correct agenda taking precedence over civil liberties, I saw voting for Hillary was the right thing to do. The responsible thing to do. I greatly respect her intelligence and believe, like Obama she makes calculated decisions with the best interest of the American people in mind.

If they wanted to vote Trump in spite of this conning, I was OK with that, but I was really physically burdened by my disgust for misinformation tipping the scales of the election in a conman's favor. This scary result became a fait accompli for me once Nate Silver's algorithms gave him a one in three chance (I also counted the states where Trump was leading two days before the election and it added up to well over 270, before it dropped a little the day of the election). I was not some kind of soothsayer; the writings were on the wall and Brexit made it clear in my mind not to trust any lead short of 10%. The media still hasn't caught up to the sentiment of the people and clearly, they don't know anything.

In some misguided vow of solidarity for Hillary, the media even ignored Julian Assange's Russian State sponsored explanation of Hillary's complicity in the Saudi Arabian government's funding of ISIS. Though Assange was clearly on a personal vendetta and the email leak was old news, it wasn't hard to see the irony in the state funding ISIS, funding the Clinton Foundation to a tune of 25 million, a few years after purchasing 60.5 billion dollars in arms from the US State Department.

While the mainstream media chose to ignore the power of his words, "Killary's" enemies on Facebook ran wild with it, still curiously much less than Benghazi. I kept telling Trump supporters there are real things to criticize Hillary for you don't have to find fake reasons. Never mind the Arab Spring that took place under Hillary and Obama's watch that turned contained relatively stable dictatorships (some were even secular) into fertile ground for Sunni-Shia proxy wars between Iran and Saudi Arabia that became proxy wars between the US and Russia.

As I was on a crusade for truth in a world lacking in it, I began fact-checking this in American papers and The Guardian. Since Assange's assertions were in my mind indisputable, I was forced to attack his character to defend Hillary. Though I've lost a lot of respect for WikiLeaks, I see Snowden and Chelsea Manning as heroes, advocates for free speech that didn't deserve to be treated as enemies of the state for revealing the clear corruption of the US government. They were right to whistleblow on the drone bombings, incompetence and corruption in the US Military. I feel the taxpayers deserved to know the NSA and CIA were needlessly spying on millions of citizens with the cooperation of multi-billion dollar corporations. Obama and Hillary took a hard stance that this was basically treason.

In spite of this, I found before the campaign Trump called for Snowden's execution, which I believe turned a wash into a point in Hillary's favor. Who knows, maybe to galvanize the support of the Bernie voters, she might even pardon these advocates of free speech, though this was probably wishful thinking. It also wasn't hard to discern the clear motivation of Russia to get Trump elected, I can only assume to divide and weaken America.

My conspiracy lightbulbs went off, thinking of Trump's wild declaration that "NATO is obsolete," which he didn't entirely let go of in the debate when he credited himself by saying, "I'm getting a lot of credit for this," about NATO renegotiations that must have happened in his imagination. It wasn't hard to argue that Trump was wittingly or unwittingly in Putin's pocket and it's still not inconceivable. I found out that the mainstream media was already covering this, which pretty much confirmed to me Trump didn't have the judgment to lead this country. Who knows if Trump agreed to pardon Assange? Would you put it past him?

While this is all interesting conjecture, and really frightening considering Ukraine was the furthest west Putin could go in his mission to bring back the USSR—only because of the strength of NATO who you remember Trump finds pointless—it is still only conjecture. It seems that Putin wants Trump in power, and perhaps it would be unwise to ignore this considering we were on the precipice of a Cold War two years ago and the boiling tension led to America essentially being at war with Russia, while the voters remain largely ignorant.

If you keep following this line of thinking, it's also not hard to criticize Hillary's involvement in the Arab Spring, while I also shudder to consider what havoc a partnership of Trump and Putin will cause. This could very well bring on World War III and the end of Western civilization, with the US fighting against or far be it from me to say alongside Russia, as more states in the Middle East destabilize as a result of US and Russian intervention. More destabilized states will start more proxy wars between Jihadist organizations, opening a bigger floodgate of refugees into Europe from countries that get more radical by the day. Excuse the hyperbole, but this could realistically drive Europe back to the dark ages. I don't think it will, but these are trying times.

Another harrowing thought is that Saudi Arabia all of a sudden has the 3rd largest military budget, substantially bigger than Russia. Complicating the matter further, America is completely dependent on OPEC's largely Saudi Arabian oil (ever wonder why your gas price is so low?). Further, after the Iran deal, America is essentially allied with Iran against ISIS, Saudi Arabia's mortal enemy.

While the US government refuses to acknowledge stuxnet, I am not the only one who believes the Israel's Mossad and America's NSA's secret cyberwar with Iran, has a large part to do with the Iran deal that essentially made Iran our ally. When the computer virus stuxnet rigged Iran's highly developed nuclear centrifuges to fail in ways that deceived people smart enough to become nuclear physicists for months on end, Israel losing patience with the progress, released a more aggressive strain of the virus. This shamed Iran, and Iran's unpredictability made America cower.

I believe Israel was operating under the assumption that if they were discovered, this would force the US to ally with Israel and destroy the falling oil giant Iran. Instead, we've armed Iran by injecting 150 billion dollars into their economy, all but ensuring Iran will have a nuclear weapon in 9 years as Podesta's email confirms. When Republican Senator, Mark Kirk of Illinois wrote Hillary's campaign manager, "This agreement condemns the next generation to cleaning up a nuclear war in the Persian Gulf…This is the greatest appeasement since Chamberlain gave Czechoslovakia to Hitler," all Podesta could respond was "Yup." I would also argue Israel, the only ideological ally to the US in the Middle East, will be vulnerable. Though Iran was once a moderate country, that still houses many prominent Jews, the backlash to the

Shah of Iran's modernization is still alive 38 years since his overthrow. Though I'm certainly more afraid of Saudi Arabia, like the rest of the Middle East, Iran is becoming much more radical.

While I don't blame the terms of the Iran deal on Clinton — Kerry and Obama are clearly the culprits here —, I blame political correctness for the utter denial of the madness of religious monarchs fighting holy wars in the Middle East. This is the same thinking that prevented Obama from even saying, "Radical Islamic terror," and with a straight-face chose not to mention a shooting in a kosher supermarket was targeting Jews.

I don't see any clear advantage to what Obama did in the Middle East in terms of self-interest or the betterment of the world, other than Opec lowering the oil prices for the consumer and making more profit for the military industrial complex. Rather than stand up to Putin, a throwback to nationalist dictators of the past, who has his sights set on conquering the Soviet era buffer states, they chose to arm Saudi Arabia and let them dictate policies, while strengthening Iran. It seems like the only country Obama stood up to was Israel.

In the Middle East and in Russia for that matter, strength is the only things these countries respect. This grave lack of understanding of Middle East warfare is part of why people condemn Israel, though these proxy wars make the wars with Gaza and The West Bank look like tea parties. Somehow with a military budget that more than doubles every other country, America finds itself stuck in unwinnable wars and forced to cower to threats, because we are so overextended, with so few troops. It really begs the question, why don't we just leave? Every attempt to police the Middle East has only caused harm.

While it is not covered heavily in our for-profit media and most people have little connection to these places, many voters have family who fought in and continue to fight in these senseless wars with no end in sight. Despite having run as an anti-war candidate in 2008, the media darling Obama has kept us in the longest running war in the history of our nation. I had some faith Clinton was more rational on Israel, it's hard to imagine she had any answers in the region. Watching the debate, I almost forgot we were at war. Though I haven't heard a coherent plan from Trump other than his plan to let the generals do their jobs and not tell the people we're attacking that we're attacking them, I'm not sure he could do much worse.

Domestically, there is this insistence from the Democrats that everything is great, because crime is down, the Dow is at record highs and unemployment is at 5%. It's like they forgot the summer of terrorism, racial tension and police murder we just experienced. The Democrats are tone-deaf, running what would have been an excellent campaign in 1992. Their convention was great and Clinton won all three debates, but that doesn't cut it anymore when the election is won and lost on Facebook and Twitter.

She couldn't brush off the stink Trump was throwing at her. Like David Geffen did in 2008, Trump sold the narrative she was a liar, in spite of the fact he was lying through his teeth and contradicting himself every other sentence with self-assuredness and authenticity. Rather than shake up the country with big promises after instilling fear with the tone of the nation that felt like, "The American Dream is dead," Hillary laughed off the conspiracies built on half-truths Trump was spewing. Hillary Clinton was a bad candidate. After literally crying like a baby, as I woke up at 5:30 Israeli time (10:30est), when I saw that Trump was probably winning Michigan, a part of me felt everything would be OK. I started to remember what I said six months ago, when I first predicted a Trump victory and I began my crazy day of commenting on everything on Facebook, "I think I'm crying right now, but also thinking this might not be as bad as it seems. Maybe Trump will be ok. No one has any idea what he's gonna do. He's a fucking wild card. I wouldn't be surprised if he picks Hillary as his secretary of state."

He has been both a Republican and a Democrat, and would say literally anything to get elected. Someone with his pride does not want to be remembered as the guy who stirred up racial tension and violence, and destroyed the economy. He's a brilliant competitor who is clearly a lot smarter than he looks. Does he really want to screw this up?

I don't think he's racist. There won't be a ban on Muslims, or a wall to Mexico. He has much too large an ego to let the party that elected him and nearly abandoned him, dictate his policies. Explaining my positive feelings to a friend on Facebook who has rightfully pissed off, I explained my theory. Another person chimed in, "So you're saying he's lying about everything and not just most things," and I really believe that is what happened and I felt a lot better.

I was tired of defending Obama and Clinton for accomplishing things like piss-poor healthcare reform and the inevitable step of marriage equality, when the world is shambles. I had a Howard Beale moment and got tired of the bullshit, writing in a flash on my phone,

"These newscasters are so stupid. It was so clear it was going to be Trump or at least be very close. When they watch a Trump rally all they can hear is their own voice, not what he's saying and how it connects to people. The media lives in a fantasy land where they believe 5% unemployment means something when

people are making the same money they did 30 years ago. The democrats don't listen to voters who hate wall street and Obamacare, feel the racial division, the threat of radical Muslim terror and are tired of pseudo fascist politically correct ideology that is so backwards it ignores science. No one has any answers but this politics as usual bullshit isn't gonna work anymore. I think Trump is a buffoon whose policies will create huge instability (though i'm hoping he was lying as much as i thought he was to get elected), but we need to start looking at how to fix this broken system where no one trusts institutions and facts no longer matter to an electorate that feels abused by the elite."

It just became so clear to me how backwards and broken our society is. How disconnected we are from each other. How we are lied to both in the obvious conspiracy theory, "Mexicans are rapists," "Killary Clinton" way and in the way that Obama and Hillary lie to us through omission and cozy relationships with reporters. I'm tired of clear acceptance that legal bribes are part of the political process. Say what you will about Donald Trump, when Prince Alwaleed, a Saudi billionaire and big Clinton Foundation contributor rightfully chastised Trump for calling on "a ban on all Muslims entering the country until we figure this thing out," Trump fought back beautifully in a tweet.

"Dopey Prince @Alwaleed_Talal wants to control our U.S. politicians with daddy's money. Can't do it when I get elected.#Trump2016." Never mind that Trump started his business with "daddy's money." He stood up the evil powers that be, without an ounce of shame or apology, and yesterday Alwaleed congratulated Trump with his tail between his legs. Maybe this is a little bit of what America needs. We need to protect our way of life by asserting our power.

Why do the Democrats have to pick a candidate who makes your stomach turn a bit when you defend her accomplishments honestly? Processing the insanity, my righteous anger turned to acceptance. All politicians are corrupt, simply by the virtue of being part of the political system. Donald has a lot of flaws, and it still seems impossible that a reality TV star/irresponsible mogul who I knew as the host of The Apprentice and the guy who rated women and like a teenager bragged about his conquests on Howard Stern is now president, without once putting on the charade of claiming to be moral.

The world felt like it was turned upside and yet many ardent Democrats seemed like by seeing the truth of the hatred revealed by the people in front of them, there was this desire to connect with each other, learn to love each other above and in spite of our differences. We were tired of being divided as a country.

When Trump accepted the nation's highest office, I was very impressed. Though I'm preparing myself for the worst, I feel hopeful. He seemed genuinely gracious and humble, remorseful for carrying such a dirty campaign out on Clinton. By calling out for the help of his opponents, I felt he genuinely wanted to unite the country he helped divide. For the first time since I can remember, I think there's a chance that Democrats and Republicans will work together to find solutions.

(the opposite has happened)

We have strong differences in character and opinion. Despite both being spoiled children from New York, I don't think we could be more different. I'm fair skinned and he's orange. I believe in restrictions on business, while he thinks yuge tax cuts stimulate growth. I'm almost 100% certain on climate change, while he's a bit iffy on it. In spite of all this, I stand behind him. After being right about the election results, I don't think I could have been more wrong. The markets didn't crash and it doesn't look like the world is ending.

WHAT ARE THEY GONNA DO NOW? PUSSY POWER PROBLEMS AND PALESTINE

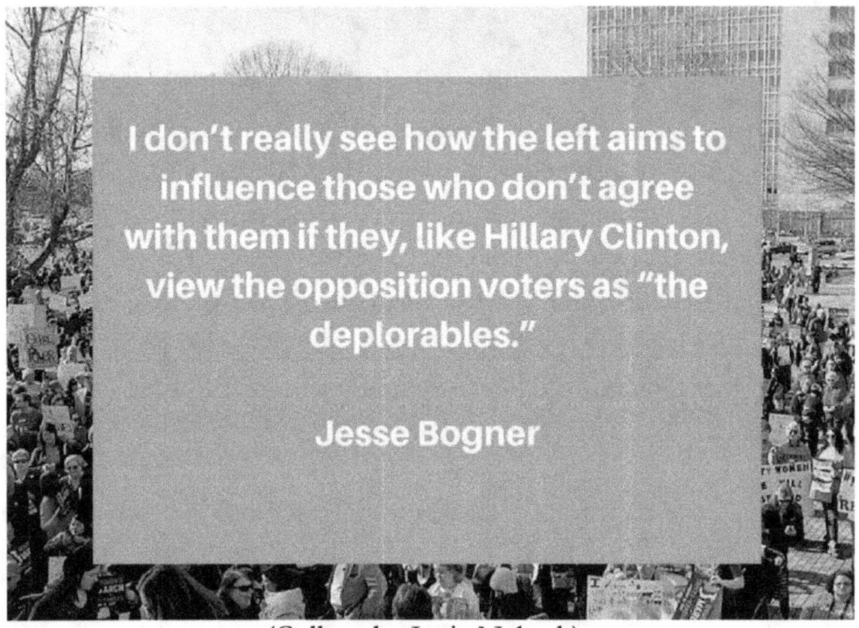

(Collage by Josia Nakash)

By all indications, the historic Women's March two weeks ago is becoming a movement. As a sane, rational person, and it feels like I'm the only one left, I love the concept of the new women's rights movement. It's a step in the right direction to protest injustice in the face of what looks like tyranny. Further, the last thing the world needs is more unwanted children. I don't think Roe v. Wade will be overturned or that Planned Parenthood will be federally defunded, but if this does happen, I'll be more than happy to use every tool at my disposal to protest it. I, like most people, think it is absurd that some people still limit female achievement in the workplace, harass women and discriminate against hiring them. I find it appalling that Hillary Clinton's gender had a part in why she wasn't elected, both from men and women. Nevertheless, I find it puzzling that 18% of women don't believe in equality across genders and 82% don't identify as feminists. Liberals must ask themselves why this is the case.

While I don't believe that Trump is a racist, or a misogynist, I also get why a lot of women hate our president on these grounds. I wouldn't want to be friends with him. What Trump said to Billy Bush about grabbing pussies and moving on Nancy O'Dell like a bitch was disgusting and pathetic. On the other hand, it was eleven years ago, he had no idea he was being recorded and it has nothing to do with his prospects as a leader. The same liberals who chastise Trump for this made the same argument when Clinton was impeached.

While I would have hoped for less morally scrupulous nominees than him and Hillary for that matter, his victory speech gave me hope that he would reverse his positions that bait racism and irrational fears. It seemed plausible that he wanted to explore suggestions from both sides of the aisle and be something closer to the centrist fiscally conservative liberal, he portrayed himself as before he started with his Obama birther nonsense.

While it's difficult to guess what Donald Trump actually cares about other than his immense wealth and beautiful women, at the top of his list is not hurting the LGBTQ community, defunding Planned Parenthood and banning abortions. Trump reluctantly said Roe v. Wade could become a state's issue in the debates. He's no ardent pro-lifer, that's Paul Ryan and Mike Pence. Trump did defund Planned Parenthood's overseas work, just as every Republican president following a Democrat has over the last 36 years when they got into office. That's all he did so far.

He did this mainly to shore up the support of the Republican Congress, who are clearly distrustful of him for being a disruptive and unpredictable former New York City liberal with a mouth like Howard Stern's Ronnie the Limo Driver. By the way, I don't find it crazy that part of the reason for this is to prioritize American issues, by making a general divestment from overseas charitable work that usually doesn't achieve anything, while creating more complex problems.

As is the case with the majority on both sides (even activists), women in their pussy hats are confused by the most basic elements of American foreign policy. They don't understand that what appears to work, or what generally seems moral has little relation to what actually works.

Without exception, what politicians say has little relation to what actually happens. With Trump, this is particularly true, because I can't think of a single thing he has been consistent on other than the wall. While I'm not crazy about the focus on deporting Mexican immigrants, who are by and large hardworking law abiding citizens, two years ago Obama was dubbed "deporter in chief" for good reason. In a confused and complex world, women are not protesting what will be the result of Trump's actions, so much as a generally molesty vibe they get from him, the blatant lying and his unpredictability.

Like Trump, the most outraged protestors live in their own version of reality. The general consensus is that Trump is a White Supremacist who hates women. While I would be hard-pressed to find someone to defend his self-proclaimed position as "the least racist person on earth," claims of Trump's racism and misogyny are wildly inflated assertions mostly based on feelings, and as Alcoholics Anonymous says, "feelings aren't facts."

He's contradictory on women. He does insult them and rate their appearance. As for racism, he insults just about everyone equally, most especially the powerful rich white men in his cabinet. His base doesn't take him seriously, the oversensitive left does. You could argue he's merely a comedian with a much less sordid history with women than Bill Clinton. Never mind the fact he put women in positions of power in his organizations decades before it was common practice. He doesn't like political correctness for its own sake. Most people on both sides don't.

The rigidity of political correctness on the left is part of the reason Trump was elected. It's certainly a big part of why 82% of women don't identify as feminists. They see the hypocrisy of the very splintered movement known as feminism, that pushes myths like the wage gap and others, based on shoddy logic and statistics.

Both Democrats and Republicans push their diametrically opposed positions with misleading information, opposing those who disagree with them vehemently, unwilling to compromise on issues, or consider the other side. When did the American mainstream liberals universally become such crybabies? As someone who has lived overseas for four years, the ideological shift towards a politically correct closed-minded victim mentality on both sides feels extreme to say the least.

One example of this, is that the 51% of women who believe abortion does more harm than good were banned from the Women's march. I don't really see how the left aims to influence those who don't agree with them if they, like Hillary Clinton, view the opposition voters as "the deplorables." Though I don't agree with them, as a white cis-gender male, I find it puzzling that half the women in America are barred from uniting women. You can't call Trump a fascist for dividing Americans and then do the same thing. As was clear to most Americans and even something a CNN correspondent accidentally blurted, "It's not a women's march. It's about liberalism." The real problem here is that liberalism has become overly rigid and illogical.

Like the incredibly unsuccessful Occupy movement, it would be rather difficult to find a goal this movement was working towards. Is it to legalize abortion nationwide? I thought that happened over 40 years ago. Rather than championing free speech and considering divergent opinions, to try and implement real changes to build a better world, liberals go to marches like this to express their discontent and then they move on. There's this assumption that if someone went to the march, and accepted the victim ideologies in absolutist terms, they did their part. If they go back, read the paper, and try to implement change they're an extremist wasting their time trying to change the world. If someone voted for Trump, or disagrees with the messages being spread, even on a factual basis, they are an ignorant racist. The unconscious mind leaves the event with the point of view, "Trump=bad, Obama=good, White people=racist hypocrites, end of story." Nothing ever changes.

One troubling problem with this simplistic narrative is that it comingles ideologically opposed struggles, because they are lumped together as enemies of Trump. Not only does Trump=bad, but Israel=bad. The Hamas apologist and "women's rights activist"

Linda Sarsour is projected as a Palestinian Bernie progressive, a Patagonia and hijab-clad woman of the people who speaks with slang like "swag," "for sure" and "straight up" in a Brooklyn accent. Her face was plastered everywhere at the Women's march in a Shepard Fairey poster of her in an American flag hijab.

(Source: theamplifierfoundation.org/wethepeople)

Though her religion and the Palestinian territories forbid abortion (and might I add gives light sentences for honor killings, information which Sarsour worked to censor from America), she was the person who made the announcement to bar pro-life women from attending the event. The media marginalizes all critique of this obvious contradiction as alt-right and racist. While I applaud her stances on abortion, gay rights, etc., those stances are mostly contrary to her religion, which arranged her marriage and brainwashed her into covering her head and body (not unlike some strains of Orthodox Judaism). Her role as an activist is highly unusual in Islam, even in Brooklyn and clearly it makes no sense for a conservative Muslim to be an advocate for women's rights and gay rights.

I suspect, as others have noted, this is an example of taqiyya, when Islam is able to present values contrary to Islamic law in service of a larger goal. It is the same argument Hamas uses when they say it's OK to use suicide bombers and kill women and children, in opposition to conventional Islamic jihad laws. Criticizing Charlie Hebdo, tweeting positives about Sharia law and Saudi Arabia's maternity leave (btw there's a very enlightening article from a Sufi Muslim woman Shireen Qudosi on why it's dangerous to blur liberal values and Saudi Arabian policy), censoring contrary opinions in defense of sharia, blatantly lying about Hamas' stance on Israel's right to exist and frequently using Zionism as a derogatory word are not qualities I want in a women's lib activist and this does not make me racist. She actively promotes the oppression of women by confusing liberals into thinking her strain of conservative Islam generally supports women speaking their minds and taking leadership roles when it does not.

Wittingly or unwittingly, the women's movement conflates women's rights with conservative Islam even when it's proselytizing for Islamist extremism. It has gotten so bad that the mainstream media shuns anyone who criticizes it, citing she was targeted by vicious Islamophobic attacks online. In the age of micro-aggression, it is anyone's best guess what these "attacks" were. In service of inclusion and freedom, liberalism has become intolerant of views that complicate politically correct agendas.

Multiculturalism has gotten in the way of looking at problems in the Arab world honestly, which often stem from highly organized extremist religious groups taking control from agendaless, disorganized secular movements and governments in places like Egypt, Gaza, Lebanon, Syria, The West Bank, Iran, Iraq, Afghanistan and elsewhere. Does this pattern sound familiar?

On the other hand, Republicans actively promote racism and xenophobia on the basis of irrational fear. Though I find the fear-mongering of the right and the travel ban ridiculous, I don't support the ignorant opinions of the Sarsour's of the world being lumped together with common sense issues like abortion.

Even though I know America will not become a sharia state any time soon, as I heard many people on the right say, I don't agree with bringing in military-aged male refugees (Why doesn't Russia, or one of the many very wealthy Arab nations who is fighting proxy wars in Syria take this responsibility, or take the Palestinians for that matter?). I always detested Bush and Obama's policy of overthrowing secular dictators based on the assumption that the Arab world wants liberal democracy, though we've seen time and again Islamist extremists always take control when democracy is force-fed. This does not make me a bad liberal.

The reason everyone in mainstream culture wants refugees is because multiculturalism and misinformed people shape public opinion. Just because Islam is a religion, does not mean its rapidly growing extremist perspectives by a lot of conservative groups not called ISIS and Al Qaeda should be given a free pass. I don't want to live in a world where the production of a cartoon of Mohammed is grounds for death and it is considered racist to support a diverse, largely secular socialist democracy like Israel. I'm tired of hearing about suicide bombers killing Americans and Israelis. Those who believe in maximal freedom, like socially progressive liberals, should be more critical of Islam. If we can't define a problem rationally for fear of offending, how will we face this global threat and the many others sure to come in a Trump presidency?

NATIONAL SECURITY AND THE FALL OF THE ROMAN EMPIRE

Let's not get into the many ways Trump's ban was illegal and thoughtless. It's over, it's all too obvious and it has been covered everywhere. Like a baby who bites and screams, Trump is testing the limits of his power with his executive orders. Since we still live in America, the president is not all powerful and there is no threat of Trump bringing back The Third Reich, even if he wanted to. The problem with Trump thoughtlessly banning immigrants is that since virtually every person with a voice in our culture who isn't paid by Rupert Murdoch opposes the ban, it opens a cavalcade of misinformed well-meaning interpretations. Angered by Trump, these liberal voices are quickly becoming intolerant of what they perceive as "intolerance." When someone as liberal as Bill Maher is branded as a racist for being critical of Islam, it's going to be impossible to fix the problem of global terrorism.

The Super Bowl was a giant PR campaign for inclusivity meant to sway public opinion away from Trump and for Islamic refugees. While it seems heartless to let Syrian children get killed by ISIS, drowning in shoddy boats as they attempt to escape, no one blinks an eye at the thousands we kill will with drone strikes. No one seems bothered by the United States arming Saudi Arabia with 115 billion dollars of weapons while they arm ISIS, or care about giving

Iran 150 billion dollars to pay similar extremist groups to fight ISIS and other Saudi proxy armies. No one is aware these are the forces really fighting in Syria and because we're allied with Saudi Arabia, we're on the wrong side and fighting our own proxy war against Russia. With emotional gusto, a campaign has been waged to accept Syrian refugees without blaming the previous administration for creating the crisis in Syria. This is Twilight Zone level mind control. For the millennials, this is Black Mirror level mind control and the terrorists are laughing at us as we brainwash the masses into loving Islam.

And if you're not being controlled by the Sharia-loving fake feminists eschewing mainstream leftist values, you are controlled by our president and his constituents.

Trump says and does so many irrational things it's hard to keep up. You don't have time to sift truth from fiction, unless you believe the media that says everything he has done is bad and wrong. It's clear the Donald is making a mockery of our press corps, who have no idea how to react. He calls real news fake news and his closest advisor is one of the leading figures in the rise of fake news to add to the confusion. Odder still, institutions like CNN and The New York Times have trafficked conspiracies. Sometimes he blatantly lies and makes crazy gaffes, while Sean Spicer and Kellyanne Conway find ways to present inarguable falsehoods as "alternative facts."

Trump's PR team is scurrying around like they work for King Joffrey, while he pisses off a different country every other day for no good reason. It seems like Trump's weakness is that no matter how many times he makes the claim he's "really smart," unlike Putin he cannot present the absurd as intelligent and reasoned. I hope he has some strategies mapped out, but it doesn't look like he does. With the left destroying itself before my eyes, maybe he doesn't have to.

I'm actually afraid to comment on what the world has become since Trump became president, because America has become a gigantic safe-space. While I don't believe in micro-aggressions, I know that if one triggers someone with them, they are branded as a bigot and a fascist. You see what happens at Berkeley when harmless alt-right provocateurs like Milo Yiannopoulos are labeled fascists. Oh, the irony. How do liberals not see that barring free speech is just as fascist as whatever Trump and Bannon are doing? How do they not see that blindly promoting the virtues of conservative Islam is supporting massive (to use a liberal world) "systemic" oppression?

While the travel ban was exercised hastily, the reaction from the left says a lot more about the state of the world than Trump's ban. Both sides are misinformed and intolerant. Like Trump voters, liberals need to see the bleak world they have inherited for what it is if there's any hope at making real change. While extolling virtues of inclusivity and truth, the left needs to begin uncovering the lies they are being fed by a superficial culture. Before the problems of the world can be cured, they need to be diagnosed properly.

LOOKING PAST THE ECHO CHAMBER: IS IT POSSIBLE TO EVALUATE TRUMP PROPERLY?

Since virtually everyone I grew up with, excepting my mother, is panicked about a lunatic absent of rational thought or a respect for reality running the most powerful nation in the world, I wanted to examine what Trump has said and pushed through so far from as neutral a point of view as possible. It is difficult to get past the obvious absurdity of such a fragile egomaniac saying ridiculous things that needlessly cause tension with anyone who disagrees with him. However, in spite of compromising the position of the press to question his highly suspicious activity, his insistence on awakening the racism of many of his supporters and his obvious lack of diplomacy (Why exactly did he provoke the Prime Minister of Australia?); it may be of some service to highlight the things Trump has done well since becoming president.

The press is so shocked by Trump's behavior, especially the confusion and misinformation he purposely spreads, they have no desire to rationally assess his actions. This only gets worse as he begins banning all the once trusted media outlets from The White House. Every conclusion on Trump in the media is born out of fear and the assumption of the worst. Though there's no doubt Trump is a real danger to the future of America and the world, Trump rightfully accuses the media of trafficking conspiracy and conjecture (ironically, because he's the king of conspiracy and conjecture). It is my belief we must drown out the propaganda from Trump and the media in order to properly assess if the world as we know it is ending.

The main premise we need to start with is that what normal politicians say publicly (especially when they run for high office) and what they accomplish bear little relationship to each other. In some cases, this is due to overly optimistic declarations in service of galvanizing support, or the administration blatantly lying. Though more times than not, overwhelmed by corporate interests, complexities and unforeseen problems, presidents are forced to compromise their promises and wishes. For instance, Obama like Trump, ran as an antiwar president. He also vowed to protect the privacy and human rights. He won the Nobel Peace Prize in 2009 for creating a persona as a peaceful leader. As of today, we are still fighting in Iraq and Afghanistan, we are largely responsible and deeply invested in a war in Syria with no end in sight, Guantanamo is still open and the NSA needlessly spies on millions of Americans all but ensuring the net is too wide to actually catch terrorists.

Aside from the obvious points that Obama was thoughtful, intelligent and on the same side as the media, this begs the question why Obama given such benefit of the doubt. Obama's relationship with the mainstream media was cordial. Only in rare instances were Obama's policies questioned very much. On the Iran deal, The White House blatantly pushed a media supported propaganda campaign to curry favor with the media with the use of an "echo chamber" of misinformation that bullied anyone with less than full-fledged support into being cast as a neoconservative warmonger (which is exactly what his administration really was, though I don't think he wanted it that way when he was elected). In reality, the money Iran received in the deal is being used to strengthen the

Iranian military, who are fighting a proxy war with Saudi Arabia in Syria, Yemen, Lebanon, Pakistan, Bahrain and Iraq that I don't see ending before Iran has legal nuclear capabilities in eight years.

Unlike Obama, the media assumes the worst of Trump, mostly for good reason and his opposition to the fourth estate. They are actively at war with him. This war is a reaction to Trump's insistence on lying and calling any critique of him fake news, but he is not solely to blame for this. The media has been extremely biased post-Reagan, but started to get really bad sometime during W's administration. As a reaction to the Murdoch Empire's success with the dissemination of misinformed opinion packaged as news and Bush's obvious incompetence and conflicted interests, the mainstream media became just as partisan as Fox. This is part of the reason Trump has had so much success calling out the media as fake news. It may shock you, but more people trust Trump than the media.

Trump chose to drown out the media establishment by currying favor to the wildly popular citizen journalist movement that Andrew Breitbart cultivated with the rise of the tea party movement and the trollers that support them by trafficking in conspiracy. With Breitbart's closest advisor and successor Steve Bannon running the Trump administration, the war with the partisan media is finally shifting in favor of the right. Trump is willfully destroying institutions, repealing and replacing. Only God knows if this has a chance of repairing the strongest nation in the history of humanity, but I wouldn't dismiss the strategy altogether.

The media is playing into Trump's hands by blatantly creating false narratives based on things Trump didn't really say. One example is the Sweden thing. When he said look at what happened in Sweden yesterday, he was exhausted and referring to some report he saw on

Fox news. He didn't make up a terrorist attack, but it worked for him in spite of how stupid the media tried to make him look. The genius of Trump drawing attention to Sweden is that there was near certainty there would be stuff to report on during the refugee crisis, if the media looked closely enough. Now the story ends up scaring the country into not wanting to take in fundamentalist refugees, which I believe is a real threat to American culture and security.

While I hate his methods at first glance, Trump is able to shift public attention for a sensible stance by removing his opposition. He understood that Obama was unable to get the public behind him with the press in his favor, so there is no point in bothering with them. In every instance Trump is able to make his own terms, regardless of truth in a post-fact world. By not caring about the truth or the politically correct party line he can open up new ways of thinking. Now we can process things differently, reconsider the failures of the past. Maybe to build something great you need to destroy it first. In my view, it's too early to judge.

EVIL VS. EVIL VS. EVIL VS. EVIL: TRUMP'S FOOLISH DECISION TO FIGHT SYRIA

	ASSAD REGIME	**"MODERATE REBELS"**
Orientation	Secular program, modernist, overcentralized state	Sharia, theocratic state similar to Saudi Arabia
Regime Type	Autocratic, but nominally democratic, with standard elections	Islamofascism, Explicitly refuse democracy
Women	Full rights (incl. MPs)	Submission
Troups	58-70% Sunnis, rest Alawis, Druze, (some) Christians	~100% Sunnis
Support	Russia, Iran, Hezbollah, (now) Egypt	Al Qaeda, Salafis-Wahabis, Qatar, UAE, Saudi Arabia, Turkey, US State department (pre-Donaldo), some Europeans
Casualties	Allegedly hits civilians	Allegedly target civilians
Treatment of Minorities	Favorable	Submission to Infidel/Dhimmi status. Openly beheads Alawis
PR	No PR outside of Russia Today and similar outlets	MSM journos (s.a. WP, NYT), think tanks & overactive PR firms financed by Qatar- Saudi Arabia

(Chart by Nassim Nicholas Taleb: medium.com)

The narrative of taking out the evil Assad to the merry band of
rebels is a gross oversimplification. Assad's soft fascism is evil,
but not nearly as evil as Islamist fundamentalism, according to the
great economic philosopher Nassim Nicholas Taleb, whose house
was blown up by Assad's father when his grandfather voted against
him (for Bashir) in Lebanon's parliament. His perspective, which I
share is that "You do not compare Assad's regime to the Danish or
Norwegian governments, but to the alternative." America points to
an unproven and difficult to believe chemical weapon
attack (difficult to believe given that Assad is no dummy) as
impetus to fight an unwinnable war with no foreseeable end.
Rather than watch the above video, if you want to understand the
conflict look at Taleb's chart describing the conflict on the
previous page.

Since we gave Iran 150 billion dollars to not build nuclear weapons,
Iran is free to fund and fight with Syria to preserve Shia Islam, as
eight proxy wars are fought in six different countries. While I tend
to prefer moderate Shia Islam (what is practiced in Syria by the
Alawi elites and overwhelmingly in Iran) to Sunni Islam
(particularly Wahhabi Saudi extremism), Iran and Syria are both
jihadist states and in a vacuum evil. Assad is a dictator who was
nearly overthrown, so he killed his non-violent adversaries in 2011.
This is exactly what totalitarian dictators with their image planted
on every street corner do.

Now let's take a look at our allies. According to npr, 1/3 of the
rebels support ISIS. These are not proxies of the nonviolent Arab
Spring protesters. 60% are Islamist jihadists as of 2015. Given the
source, I assume this is a charitable estimate. They found 25% to
not belong to an ideology (code word for mercenaries often trained
by the USA or liars). Without even thinking about ISIS, Assad's
main adversaries, "the rebels" mostly believe in jihad, the

infallibility of the Quran and the Wahhabi Imam, Abdul Rahman Al-Sudais, that largely governs Saudi Arabia. Their political ideology is being spread all over the Middle East, Europe and America. It is Osama Bin Laden's worldview. Aware of the problem, and the fact that the weapons and training we offered to fight ISIS are being directed to ISIS and Al Qaeda either through negligence or to combat Assad, Senator Rand Paul was trying to push a bipartisan bill to stop arming terrorists a month ago.

Aside from galvanizing support at home, I have no idea what Trump is thinking. He definitely won the PR battle, which legitimizes him with the leftists he needs to pass his exclusively tax-payer funded, trillion-dollar infrastructure plan. One of the main reasons I supported Trump (admittedly only after he was elected) was because he was going to stay out of Syria. He was different than the neocons and Hillary who were going to start World War 3, who are now applauding Trump's leadership.

Purveyor of fictional news (not a Trump thing, he was suspended for making up stories), Brian Williams, has a fetish for "the deep state" and the beauty of missiles.

Establishing a no-fly zone seems like a no-brainer, but do we really want to be at war with Russia, Syria, Hezbollah and Iran? Did we really have to provoke Assad? If it was us alone, I could definitely stomach it, not that I think just because Assad is essentially a Western-style dictator, he is any worse than a Communist dictator, or the many Islamist dictators in the region. I do believe in standing up to evil, but there are degrees of evil. Our side is much worse in this war. Saudi Arabia is the crux of the rise of Islamist extremism, who along with Qatar funded ISIS and indirectly funded the 9/11 hijackers.

While at first, I reverted to the "this is a really complex issue and the government must know something we don't," I came to the conclusion this war is an idiotic proposition, especially after the Iran Deal (Obama's other legacy) that greatly strengthened our enemy and ideological enemy Iran. Iran, the "moderate" nation that executes homosexuals, whose world-class film directors blame us for "the racist Muslim Ban" at the Oscars, while they arm, fund and fight with Assad. And of course, like all the obscenely wealthy underpopulated gulf states they fight proxy wars against, Iran refuses to take in refugees or the "equally oppressed" Palestinians. To make matters worse, Trump is standing proud with the Jordanian King Abdullah II, who blames Israel for the instability of the Middle East without offering refuge to the "victims" in Gaza and The West Bank even though 70% of his population is Palestinian. Trump should be ashamed of himself when he buys his daughter's Passover chametz today.

JAMES COMEY AND MARINE LE PEN: CASUALTIES OF THE WAR BETWEEN NEOLIBERAL AND DEPLORABLE

May 9th, 2017: As James Comey gave a speech to his LA office, the news on the TVs announced his firing. Comey thought he was a victim of an elaborate prank. Amidst the laughter, he was taken to the FBI offices seven blocks away by Trump's personal bodyguard, who read James Comey a matter-of-fact and sarcastically gracious letter that only Trump could have conceived:

Dear Director Comey:

I have received the attached letters from the Attorney General and Deputy Attorney General of the United States recommending your dismissal as the Director of the Federal Bureau of Investigation. I have accepted their recommendation and you are hereby terminated and removed from office, effective immediately.

While I greatly appreciate you informing me, on three separate occasions, that I am not under investigation, I nevertheless concur with the judgment of the Department of Justice that you are not able to effectively lead the Bureau.

It is essential that we find new leadership for the FBI that restores public trust and confidence in its vital law enforcement mission.

I wish you the best of luck in your future endeavors.

Donald J. Trump

Cameras followed Comey to a private plane. Within a few hours, the left and the establishment neoliberal class, in a state of genuine confusion (as they wanted Comey gone a few months earlier) theorized about the timing of the dismissal, suggesting Trump was sabotaging the Russian collusion investigation.

May 10th, 2017: Trump met with Russian Foreign Minister Sergey Lavrov and Russian Ambassador to the US Sergey Kislyak at the White House. Kislyak is the ingeniously evil Putin loyalist that led to Mike Flynn's ousting. Making matters even more odd, Trump was aided by Hillary's ally, Henry Kissinger, you know Nixon's skirt-chasing Secretary of State, who invented the globalist policy of making strange bedfellows (Mao, Soviet Union General Secretary Brezhnev, Pinochet) in the service of a cybernetic theory of balance of power between nations called REALPOLITIK. I guess you could call this trolling of the highest order.

(Collage by Jesse Bogner)

James Comey is the status-quo incarnate. He is the encapsulation of everything that is wrong in the world. When everything is politicized, including a leftist initiative to make choke-proof hot dogs and a march for leftist policies and the death of religion masked as a march for science, it becomes increasingly difficult to trust those in government making claims of objectivity. Post-Bush number 2, the FBI has been endowed with extraordinary powers. The hearsay is that Comey used those powers to intimidate opposition.

On the surface, he injected himself into last November's historic election calling for the Democrats to demand his dismissal. First, he said Hillary was under investigation, then acknowledged the illegality of the email scandal, exaggerating the number of emails and the illegality, before saying Hillary broke the law. Since in his view he deemed her intentions as pure, he decided there was no reason to prosecute. I was not aware that purity of intention was a reason for legal immunity. Trump's calls to "lock her up," if immoral, were probably legally substantial.

When he started to question Trump's credibility with unsubstantiated Russia collusion stories, aside what is clearly known about Russia Today playing a role in Trump's election, he became an arm of the left protecting the powers of his institution that the Bannon arm of the White House want to by all indications expand, as long as they're not being used to destroy Trump's initiatives. The problem has nothing to do with the Trump administration, but a refusal to support Trump publicly.

James Comey has no business in such a delicate position of power. He shouldn't be campaigning for legislation or political candidates, while he extols his own virtues, describing the moment each day when he looks to a picture of Martin Luther King Jr. as a reminder not to abuse his powers, like the FBI had to King half a century before. He's not running for office. No one wants to see the human side of an intelligence director. He's supposed to feign neutrality.

Aside from being a drama queen, like both sides of the aisle these days, Comey has little respect for the law or due process. Trying to push ideological aims, he has a Machiavellian devotion to his own interests in spite of the socially liberal virtue signaling. That's why the FBI, along with the CIA and NSA, practiced tracking the digital records of millions of Americans and Obama's cowardice is why they won't clamp down on the search to a smaller number to have a chance in hell of combatting actual terror suspects.

A few years ago, Comey lied about the Surveillance States of America by suggesting that since the tech and phone companies are the ones storing the information, the culture has changed. Phone records are requested routinely, but God knows what's going on. They're unaccountable, unelected and by all accounts unsuccessfully targeting terrorists, as they take away our civil liberties. General Michael Hayden below illuminates that the only change post-Snowden is voluntary in line with an Obama PR policy, "and by the way we (intelligence community) can change our mind at any time…"

This of course is not a concern of Trump. He wants the unconstitutional power of the intelligence communities that Obama had and he wants to push the petal to the metal, but it was highly unusual for him to fire an FBI director.

Both James Comey and French fascist candidate for Prime Minister Marine Le Pen feel emblematic of our time, wherein the powers that be seek to take down dangerous forces of change. After being nudged left for decades by the elites, the far right (including populists like Trump who are in reality incompetent centrists) begin to fight back. No one in the center has been willing to fight for decades, since in America when a Republican politician insults a Democrat, he calls him a socialist and the Democrat proceeds to call the Republican a racist.

When normal people watch Trump talk, they see he is not racist. He started campaigning on the issues that could change these peoples' lives for the better and they started to listen. They see the hypocrisy of a stuck-up media that takes a man who's clearly half-joking half the time at face value. They know Trump is a conman and they don't care. "He's conning for America first you libtard!"

While Le Pen was the leader of a party once led by an ardent Holocaust denier in the bygone era of 2002, who happened to be Marine's father, Trump said something about Mexicans send rapists across the border once. Not exactly equivalent evils. Still, they are both nationalist leaders and judged with the same brush in the media. They are threats to the politically correct order of identity politics that shifts the nature of acceptable thought and opinion without opposition, for the opposition is afraid of being called racist.

In today's world, policies don't matter as much as perceptions. Though I don't think Trump is racist misogynist, he's assumed to be one. He is a narcissist, who by nature of running a business that runs like a dictatorship is confused when laws cause roadblocks, because he doesn't know what the laws are yet. The constitution and liberal alarmists make sure he doesn't take advantage of the executive branch that Obama and Bush successfully strengthened, while the country nearly destroyed itself.

The elites across party lines are joining together in spite of huge ideological differences to take down the likes of Trump, Farage, Le Pen and Wilders. Look at the #resistance movement, where neocon millionaires and Hillary Clinton fight with Upper Middle-class acolytes of pseudo-intellectual Chomsky, Zinn, Said and Butler spouting professors, while feeling the weight of their oppression like they were in the *THE HANDMAID'S TALE*. These Nationalist leaders are so repugnant to the global neoliberal elites and leftists, mainly on a personality front that they sling their names through the mud with misinformation and exaggeration.

Not only do they have ultimate authority over 90% what is taught (explicitly teaching what to think instead of how to think), read, watched, listened to and promulgated with advertising, the elites make it their business to fight dirty. They share so many common interests (open borders for cheap labor, basic universal income to sustain commerce in an age of automation, identity politics, political correctness, market stability) that this group will be the source of autocracy in America if it ever comes to that. Since the left is entirely blind to their own errors, they don't see that they put together a team of who most of the country actively hates. They still believe this will defeat Trump in 2020.

In Hillary's attempts to appeal to the youth, all she has done is inherit the millennial victim mentality, complete with zero self-awareness. Trump is an assault on everything these earth-toned clad stoner paid protestors wear (I have no evidence of this highly likely Soros injection of money for protest, I just love triggering militant liberals off at this point!). It's so clear people are disturbed by Trump's taste and demeanor more than anything else. The right doesn't care, because Trump wants the media to criticize him for Comey, so he can illustrate how hypocritical his opposition is.

Nassim Nicholas Taleb
Published by Nassim Nicholas Taleb [?] · Just now · 🌐

The *establishment* composed of journos, BS-Vending talking head well-formulated verbs, bureaucrato-cronies, lobbyists-in training, Ne Yorker-reading semi-intellectuals, image-conscious empty suits, Washington rent-seekers and other "well thinking" members of the elites are not getting the point about what is happening and the ster their arguments. People are not voting for Trump (or Sanders). Peo just voting, finally, to destroy the establishment.

Neoliberalism and automation created huge gaps in income and culture. While the left pushes their "regressive left" critical theory laden agenda, the middle class sees their paychecks shrinking and their bridges collapsing. They see the American Dream dying in their dilapidated houses, praying for their kids to get off opiates. The left sees Le Pen and Trump voters as racist, when in reality they are angry that they can't get a new car or take their kids on vacation, while paying three times Mitt Romney's 9% effective tax rate. They want to burn the government down and start from scratch, or just push the clock back 30 years. It has become a war between not so much ideals, but a desire to maintain something resembling the status quo (neoliberals) and righteously indignant bad taste (deplorables).

This week two major battles were won on both sides. The 39-year-old Macron butchered Marine Le Pen, a nationalist-socialist. The irony was not lost that Hitler had the same basic platform as Le Pen. President Trump fired CIA director James Comey with the inconceivable reasoning that he was unhappy with the way Comey handled the Clinton email investigation. The media played this clip, where Trump honors Comey's bravery, of course making Trump look ridiculous.

They do neglect the part of the story just afterwards, not for lack of knowledge, but a conscious or unconscious decision to assume every decision Trump makes is the biggest scandal since Watergate. Everything is Nixonian. Trump was upset with Comey for clearing Clinton of charges that even Comey said were valid. Since it looked like he was going to lose the election, he was blaming the rigged system that Comey represented.

With that said, the timing makes absolutely no sense. Given the learning curve of Trump and his administration, my guess would be a combination of a sense of disloyalty from Comey and incompetence on the part of Trump. The left sees this as more evidence of the Trump-Russia collusion. There is no credible evidence for this, or the Russians hacking Clinton's email, but the truth no longer matters.

So, what really happened this week? One old elite mad with abuse of power lost his job and the youngest leader of France since Napoleon Bonaparte took the reins of government with old-school establishment elitism and a 64-year-old wife. The story is not so much the story. The story is about perception.

Perception management is the term for a foreign power gaining influence (or the US to a foreign power) to affect the beliefs and values of a country, you know, influence elections. While I have no doubt Russia Today and Eastern European for-profit memedroppers played some role in the election, I guess you would have to call that a trade-off of living in a largely ignorant country that is part of a global society. I'm much more concerned with the perceived threat of Russian perception management being used as a vessel to be biased to the point of conspiratorial about everything Trump does.

While the little I know about Marine Le Pen is horrifying, I'm more dismayed by the new trend of Conservative elites and liberals uniting against common enemies. An uninspired choice, Macron is like a young Hillary Clinton with an old wife. The guy is socially liberal in the corporatized globalist politically correct identity politics way and fiscally neoliberal. While many people abstained from voting, Macron had nearly as many conservatives voting for him as liberals.

America changed. France wanted to stay the same. Neither country seems better off. Macron is a gigantic victory for the order of institutional power, marking one of the rare times in modern history where all "sensible" Conservatives and Liberals united to take down a common populist threat. Basically, what journalists and conservative elites thought would happen to Trump actually happened to Le Pen. Does this say something about the countries or the tone of the interconnected global society? This war trumps ideology, religion, country and confuses everything that you thought you knew about both parties.

Comey is a confusing mess of contradictions and a mess of contradictions for Trump. Trump is President but cannot exercise his powers, or gain anyone's trust, even after passing just about everything the Democrats wanted and getting nothing in return. I assume firing Comey was trolling the Democrats, but if he was earnestly trying to garner their support, he should just give up. As I wrote last week in my science article, "Trump could employ every person in America at double the salary, broker peace in the Middle East and the elites would still be hounding him about Putin and "lies" which are almost always merely exaggerations." The only principle is that no one has any principles.

EVIL LOSERS

Trump's characterization of terrorists as "evil losers" is his best quality. He sees through BS and takes down BS artists who want to destroy the West. In spite of his Wharton pedigree, Keynesian economics never penetrated his skull, let alone cultural Marxism or queer theory. Though in practice he's had some trouble thus far, his intention is to put American interests above foreign interests, which in spite of the Democratic party's position is the job of the president.

Obama read and internalized critical theory by the Palestinian godfather of the belief that cultural appropriation is a micro-aggression and hate speech is worse than violence, Edward Said. Cultural Marxism, the concept that we live in societies composed of victim and oppressors is his absolute truth. This is not because Obama is a Muslim, it's because he's an atheist. This atheism creates the need for an irrational belief system, as humans are emotional animals and do not see meaning in pure reason. This is why it seems perfectly reasonable to someone like Obama to accept a worldview from Said, whose biggest influence was Frantz Fanon who famously believed "killing a European is killing two birds with one stone, eliminating in one go oppressor and oppressed: leaving one man dead and the other man free."

While I am against the legacy of Imperialism, it's hard to lead the

Western World when a not so inconsequential part of your heart wishes for the Westerners to bludgeoned to death for their past oppression overseas. The degree of the "oppression" or the fact that the oppression of minorities in America has more to do with economics, the dissolution of poor families (disproportionately affecting African Americans) and educational inequity than racism is of course of no consequence. Jews and Muslims encounter just as much, if not more racism and thrive economically in America. And the Jews of the Middle East have thrived in spite of being attacked on all sides with a dearth of natural resources, making the left assume they stole this economy stability. Further, since Palestine was a colony of England from 1917–1948 (declared to become an independent Jewish State in 1922 in the league of Nations, 26 years before its actual statehood), Obama views Israel as a colonial power and oppressor, ignoring the fact that many Jews were murdered by the real oppressor, the British empire, when they tried to emigrate to Palestine during and after the Holocaust.

While Obama publicly did little to denounce Israel, he worked against Israel's interests with the Iran deal and abstained from a vote that declared all settlements "by the occupier Israel," including those built before Israel was a state in "flagrant violation of international law." What this means is that 2 million Muslims are allowed to live in Israel, but Jews are not allowed to live in Palestine when peace is made according to international law.

Under the radar, Obama gave billions in "humanitarian aid" to Palestine that was used to build rockets and tunnels, a state that pays the families of suicide bombers a living wage and names schools and hospitals after these "martyrs." Additionally, he made it very difficult for an Israeli to get a work visa or US citizenship, as evidenced by the state department refusing to grant a Visa to Gal Mekel when the Mavericks wanted to extend the Israeli point guard's contract. All in all, Obama hated Israel.

Trump doesn't have this problem. He genuinely seems in awe of Israel, though maybe a bit disappointed by its lack of Saudi grandeur. He does have the problem of dealing with the mess that Bush and Obama made in the Middle East. He has the other problem of not wanting to provoke Saudi Arabia so they'll keep buying our overpriced weapons to help maintain the 15% uptick in the Dow since his election.

He also, not unlike Obama, is burdened with an ego unable to ignore the hero's welcome the Saudis gave him. We no longer need Saudi oil, but we do need them to buy our weapons, which will fund more terrorists in Saudi Arabia's fight with Iran, while they spend billions building Wahhabi temples across the world that aim to Islamize Europe. Further, Trump's ego compels him to pursue the "ultimate deal" in Israel, establishing his greatest dealmaker in the history of the world legacy. Peace in the Middle East is big-league. It makes Trump Tower and the Taj Mahal look like small potatoes.

Like every President in modern history, Trump made nice with the Saudis and laughably proclaimed to fight ISIS' terror with the government that funded ISIS, days before claiming to fight terror with the guy who funded the Munich Massacre of 1972, who presides over a terror state, who promotes the idea that "We welcome every drop of blood spilled in Jerusalem… they |Israel| have no right to desecrate them with their filthy feet and we won't allow them to."

While I don't love Trump's alliance with Saudi Arabia, as they are protectors of Israel for the time being, I don't see much of an alternative. I like his decision to proclaim that Iran will never get a nuclear weapon, but the expectation that Saudi Arabia, a radicalized sharia state with the 3rd largest military budget in the world is going to fight terrorist groups they fund and train with us by the way (intentionally or not) is insane. Just as insane as not mentioning the terror experienced by Israel in his speech to the Saudis and his underplaying of the role of Islam in the terror plaguing the world (that mostly affects Muslims) and the oppression of women (genital mutilation, forced child marriages, burkhas, ½ a person under Islamic law, not allowed to drive in Saudi Arabia, et al.).

On his podcast yesterday, Ben Shapiro argued that the world views the conflict between Israel and Palestine as a territorial conflict when it is in reality a religious one. When Palestine had control over Jerusalem it was used as a launching point for attacking Israel, like they did in the Six Day War of 1967. When Palestine was offered 46% of the land in the Palestine Mandate 1947 (not including the 78% of the entire landmass given to Jordan), they decided to start a war with the Jews. Before the wall to Gaza, thousands were massacred on the streets from 2000–2003. The aim of Hamas, the partner in Abbas' coalition government who controls Gaza is to eradicate every Jew from the face of the earth.

So, while I'm happy Trump visited Israel, I'm a little disturbed by his changing opinion of Islamic fundamentalism when it suits his interest. He's starting to sound like Obama-lite, when he a little too wholeheartedly supports the evil people he's forced to ally with. The danger of this is not policy, but a swing from people even on the right to view radical Sunni Islam as tolerant when it is a dangerous, backward political ideology that aims to destroy us, like literally. Islam, like all religions needs to be tolerated, but the most backwards and powerful sect of Islam that is practiced in Saudi Arabia needs to be recognized for what it is. It is *The Handmaid's*

Tale, what the #resistance movement is named after. In spite of what #resistance fighter Chelsea Clinton says, the word Islamophobia, is a tool to avoid looking at the reality that a minority of Muslims — but somewhere in the hundreds of millions — sympathize with jihad and hold values incompatible to the West, while they aim to take over the West. If she or her future anti-Israel, hypocritically half-Jewish spawn is one day president, I may have to disappear for a while.

IRAN, ISRAEL AND THE LIGHT

If the Iran Deal has an historical equivalent, it is the moment in 1938 when Neville Chamberlain agreed to allow Hitler to absorb Austria into his evil empire. Just as Hitler violated the terms of his negotiations with Britain by invading Poland and starting World War II which resulted in the death of 55 million, it is just a matter of time before Iran tries to wipe out Saudi Arabia and eventually Israel, rather than just funding terrorist proxy armies in Syria and elsewhere.

When Trump lambasts that the Iran Deal is "the worst deal in history," he is not, as is often the case, filling the room with hot air. Though by all accounts Iran has stuck to the letter of the law with its deal to stop enriching most of its uranium and giving up 75% of its centrifuges, the 150 billion dollars injected into its economy directly plus the incalculable benefit of lifting sanctions has done little to make Iran a friend of the West. All Iran has done is escalate the conflict in Syria and six other countries by using its Iran deal acquired economic strength to fund Shia terrorist armies. This is why I find it so puzzling that the neoliberal establishment countries of France, Germany and the UK are so against reworking the terms of the deal, even as Iran creates proxy armies against their ally Saudi Arabia, while threatening the security of Israel.

Iran has become like so many other agendas of the left, some sort of sacred cow. While many people rightly see the Iran Deal as what

Trump would call "a disaster," the media looks at any critique of "Obama's great diplomatic victory" as conspiratorial. Even though the press has covered in great detail how Obama adviser Ben Rhodes created an echo-chamber in the press to garner support for a largely negative negotiation wherein America is giving up 150 billion dollars to and empowering one of the world's most repressive regimes that just happens to fund Hezbollah, this echo chamber still exists.

To the left, anything that Obama accomplished is a net positive, regardless of the results. While I do like that Iran does not seem to developing nuclear weapons, they will be in eight years when the deal expires, or whenever they decide the time is right to rather than just destabilize the Middle East to make a full-scale assault to dethrone Saudi Arabia as the leading power. While I also find Saudi Arabia's domestic policies as well as their desire to further the agenda of the most repressive form of Islam called Wahhabism throughout Europe appalling, I am a practical person.

The most pressing need at the moment is Israel's security and with four rockets from Iran's ally Syria happening to land in the Golan Heights of Israel last week, it seems like an inevitable conclusion that instability in the Middle East driven by a holy war between Iran and Saudi Arabia will eventually weaken the state of Israel. I don't think strengthening these two powers will ever net positive results. Israel needs to stand firm with Trump and question the status quo as the world does everything in its power to condemn the one liberal democracy in the Middle East.

What we learn from Iran and the sad state of affairs when the West is forced to ally themselves with their ideological enemy Saudi Arabia, is that the world is in an irresolvable crisis. Though Israel's one desire is to remain safe and neutral in this *balagan* (fiasco), somehow Syria is presenting to the United Nations that Israel is to blame for the instability in the region. When it comes to Israel, the level of irrational thoughts and blame is never ending. No military or political solution will ever save Israel as long as the public sentiment views Israel as an oppressive war criminal apartheid regime, when in reality they are surrounded by the least humane powerful nations in the world and only fighting for survival. With the world fighting Israel above rational explanation, it is Israel's purpose to unite as one and fulfill the ideological mission of our ancestors to be a light to the world. This will only happen if Israel realizes the ideals of love and unity it was founded on 1948, because no matter what *detentes* Israel agrees to with the world, the world will continue to blame the one Jewish state for everything in the Middle East. Rather than fight the world, it is the responsibility of Israel to fight the selfishness of human nature and come to a common prayer to build peace in the world together through our selflessness and unity. Only if is Israel is united will the world see the state as an example instead of an enemy.

IRAN PROTESTS SIGNAL SEA CHANGE AND HOPE FOR THE MIDDLE EAST

Still seemingly under the control of Obama's echo chamber in the coverage of Iranian policy, it took days for the mainstream media to catch up to the tenor of the protests. While initial reporting cited economics and unemployment as the main factor driving the discontent, anyone with a twitter account could see clearly this was an ideological protest with revolutionary undertones. As traditional liberals would jump to support an oppressed people under a totalitarian regime, Obama's alliance with the Iranian government causes a sense of dissonance from common sense reality. Iran is viewed as a friendly sophisticated nation winning Oscars and criticizing Trump's inhumane travel ban in the acceptance speech, all the while they are funding extremist Shia terrorist armies and executing homosexuals. Those who live in Iran are not at all influenced by the Obama PR campaign and have begun to fight back at the oppressive regimes ruining their lives.

Something has changed. As Lee Smith noted in tabletmag, the implication of those who stand in the streets regularly shouting "Death to Israel and Death to America," shouting "Death to Ayatollah," taking off burkas at risk of their welfare and lives means something is shifting fundamentally. Iran is an odd country. A lot of wealthy, highly educated (including women) people live there. In the 70s, Tehran looked like a modern secular city, but today their Supreme leader is the Ayatollah Khomeini, successor to the Ayatollah who introduced Sharia-lite after overthrowing the

Shah of Iran. Iran is a place with a lot of potential for reform, but the Iran deal shored up the power of the fundamentalist leader who already according to Reuters controls about 90 billion dollars in assets mostly from property seizures.

The response to the protests is largely what you would expect from a totalitarian regime: social media blackouts, hundreds of arrests, and twelve murdered protestors. Interestingly, it hasn't made anyone back down. The protests are spreading all around the country and have been supported by the US government. Trump's allegiance with the oppressed protestors is a brilliant move. Obama, against the grain of the liberal MO of protecting oppressed peoples, failed to help Iranian people, just as he failed to help other innocents fighting oppressive regimes during the Arab Spring.

Similar Green protests against the election of famous Holocaust denier Mahmoud Ahmadinejad occurred in 2009, while Obama began his strategy of strengthening Iran in the Middle East with the Iran Deal. A weakened power with strict sanctions on the verge of the type of revolution liberals are supposed to champion, for some reason that I can't wrap my head around, Obama wanted to shift power in the Middle East to Iran. Him and national security adviser Ben Rhodes were literally feeding understaffed newspapers with no foreign correspondent's stories false narratives about Iran, such as the negotiations did not begin with Ahmadinejad in 2008, before Obama was president, to push his deal through. It was revealed in 2016, Rhodes sold Obama's false narratives easily, since, "Most of the outlets are reporting on world events from Washington. The average reporter we talk to is 27 years old, and their only reporting experience consists of being around political campaigns. That's a sea change. They literally know nothing."

As anyone with any knowledge of the Iranian government (or basically anyone over the age of 27) could have told you, the deal has not been very good for the Middle East or the Iranian people. The 150 billion dollars that Iran is receiving from Obama's historic deal has not trickled down to its oppressed people. Iran has huge economic problems, including 40% unemployment for young people. Instead, the Iran deal money has been spent on proxy armies, a nice word for terrorist organizations like Hezbollah and Hamas, fighting Saudi forces in Syria, Yemen, Afghanistan and elsewhere. This purportedly peacemaking Iran Deal, basically ensured the Shia states of Syria and Iran would be fighting Sunni powers like Saudi Arabia (third largest military budget in the world) until the oil money ran out or one of them obtained a nuclear weapon, which under the current structure of the deal is all but guaranteed to happen the day the deal runs out in seven years.

Trump's support of the protestors looks to be more than just a few words.

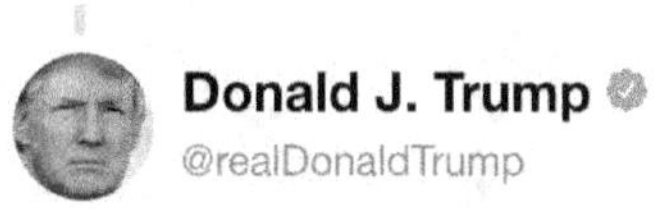

Iran is failing at every level despite the terrible deal made with them by the Obama Administration. The great Iranian people have been repressed for many years. They are hungry for food & for freedom. Along with human rights, the wealth of Iran is being looted. TIME FOR CHANGE!

4:44 AM - 1 Jan 2018

21,019 Retweets 77,243 Likes

As he's looking to back out of the Iran Deal, as anyone with a shred of human dignity would want, we might see a president who seems to be keeping his promise of wiping Isis off the map, pushing for real reform in the Middle East. Trump's threat of keeping a watchful eye on Iran, and his threats to throw out the Iran deal, seems to me like a much better reason to deserve a Nobel Peace Prize than Obama's 2008 election, as it will severely weaken Hezbollah and Hamas and enrich the lives of millions of oppressed peoples who are hamstrung by similarly bad fundamentalist religious leaders (often much worse) who care for their nation's military aims and hatred of their enemies more than the rights and welfare of their own people. As a boon for the Jewish people and democracy, it is likely to take Iran's aims off of Israel for a while.

On Culture

WE'VE ALL BECOME PARANOID WEIRDOS: HOW SCIENCE AND PSEUDO-SCIENCE BECAME DOGMA

Dogs don't have a firm concept of time, but seem to possess episodic memory. While this information is clearly interesting, knowing that a dog disciplined seven seconds after committing an error will be confused about the reason he is being punished, or that dogs recognize some difference between thirty minutes and two hours, but no difference between two and four hours is not something we comprehend. This knowledge does not help us understand what it would be like to view the world from a dog's lens. Where does the time go?

This shows us that our understanding of the world is limited, by our own perception, which we assume isn't all that different from someone else's and in broad strokes it is nearly exactly the same with some exceptions. We are not equal physically, socially or mentally and come from different environments, so our prejudices are different. But if two men look at a beautiful woman, they both see a beautiful woman. One might be drawn to this woman, while one finds her two skinny, but it's not because they see different things, it's because they have different memories and genes.

In most cases people cling to those who they have some natural inclination towards, usually based on genetic reasons I'm not qualified to describe, cultural commonalities, shared interests and common tastes. While two friends may fight for hours about how they can't believe he listens to Drake so much when Kendrick Lamar is so much better, they have a shared interest in rap. While we have differences of opinion, on the surface we see the same things.

While scientists often make statements like time doesn't exist, time is relative, free will doesn't exist, "The likelihood that we live in base reality is one in billions," and that the world only exists in our perception, these ideas are contrary to our experience. Believe it or not, all these views are widely accepted and proven by scientists aside from the simulation theory that many scientists find highly probable, though not as probable as Elon Musk's minimal certainty of 99.9999999%. When asked if science and religion can coexist Musk replied "probably not."

These accepted views are so divorced from my experience, I'm not entirely sure that I have any clear sense what these theories purport to mean. I can measure time with primitive technology and an hour feels like an hour.

Apart from my wiring that makes it feel like I'm choosing everything from the clothes I put on each morning to the words I choose writing this sentence, I've begun to embrace how little I actually control. I've questioned free will and it hasn't killed my motivation. It's made me feel more whole and compassionate by and large, when I'm not writing about politics on the internet.

Free will's nonexistence often disarms other people. It opposes the merit of religion, makes morality hard to argue for and is probably a big reason why highly intelligent highly educated atheist leftists find it hard to differentiate between good (people like evangelicals adopting 8 Ethiopian kids) and evil people (HAMAS, ISIS, I think they call it ISIL on the left, "*Salam alaikum brothers and sisters!*").

Some things are even more vague and confusing. Science gives us a glimpse of a hidden reality, where we can understand the machinations of things that are not perceptible on the surface. When someone says that time doesn't exist, does that mean that life is really like *Arrival,* where events are experienced non-sequentially? If this is the case, who has awareness of this?

It has to be the Randian uber-men controlling the virtual reality simulation. It's probably just a lark for them. If they believe in "time," they can probably simulate billions of years in what would be half a second to us backwards people who still see reality through our false conception time. Or maybe their world is so damaged by the silent killer, climate change, that they don't experience anything outside the simulation. They prefer it to reality.

It doesn't seem realistic that when I close my eyes the world disappears, or that nothing would exist without conscious beings, but who am I to argue? If I was someone else, I would experience things much differently. In a few years, we will probably be able to perceive a wildly different stream of perception without the aid of hallucinogens, on some virtual reality tip, but until then the deeper we explore science, the more questions we get and some of both the probable and improbable conclusions sound downright loopy.

If the world is a computer simulation, I have no means of confirming or denying it and if I hadn't seen *The Matrix,* this theory wouldn't have occurred to me, though the level of meaningful coincidences that have altered my life does make the concept of some intelligence beneath the surface of reality plausible.

It just doesn't make sense how this all came about. Did scientists all walk out of that Keanu Reeves film, throw out their bibles and start praying to the Wachowski Brothers? Is the sex change of these sages, now the Wachowski Sisters, why so much scholarship has been devoted to validating the transgender movement scientifically?

Just a sidebar so you know where I stand on this: It's a free country. People should do whatever they want and who cares if being a woman born with a penis is scientifically valid? It seems to have turned the antagonist Bruce Jenner into a lovely woman. What's the problem? Still, I find hormone therapy for children morally repugnant and it is important that we honestly address the 40% attempted suicide rate of transgender people. There are probably links between transgenderism and psychological disorders. I'm sorry if it offends your sense of politically correct morality. Environment is just part of the problem here. There has never been a strong link between discrimination and suicide and unhappy men don't magically become happy women.

So back to this computer simulation. Are we all being operated, or are most of us just cannon fodder for the hero? And if so, who is the hero? Wouldn't it be immoral for such a sophisticated society to build a world of so much suffering? Does the fact that we're just data in a computer program minimize the feeling of responsibility, like that episode of Black Mirror where the woman made a simulacrum of herself to be her slave? Elon Musk was not lying. This is a never-ending rabbit hole.

Thank you for your patience, but I do have one, maybe two more pressing question on my version of the planet earth. If Elon Musk really believes our lives are just virtual reality simulations, why does he work so hard making electric supercars while spending the rest of his time within the simulation figuring out how to colonize Mars? Wouldn't it seem rather pointless if he's just being operated by some spoiled kid of a future race of high-IQ humans or another species? I guess the answer is self-evident. He is being controlled by a really good player.

Only one of the nine theories of parallel universes that famed pop-science author Brian Greene waxes poetical on, Neil DeGrasse Tyson thinks there's a fifty percent probability that our world is a computer simulation, but also finds some of these other disqualifying theories interesting, in my view discounting his 50/50 belief in it. Not exactly the best science. Like me he finds the prospect of living in a simulacrum rather bleak, noting in Scientific American, "We would be drooling, blithering idiots in their presence. If that's the case, it is easy for me to imagine that everything in our lives is just a creation of some other entity for their entertainment." This irrational speculation of an advanced deity-like species toying with us on their computer, doesn't compromise Tyson's desire to "Terminate" Religion.

Bill Nye the Science Guy, whose scientific credentials is an engineering degree, is a self-identifying scientist, but now also a self-identifying philosopher in Big Think videos. He thinks the simulation thing is probable and views religion as the oppressor of scientific inquiry and discovery.

I say self-identifying as he has used faulty science to propagate the ideal that sex isn't determined by chromosomes, but as something fluid.

Though the only "scientific" evidence for this comes in the form of

Judith Butler's critical gender theory, it should probably win over a lot of working class Democrats who voted for Trump. Science, like philosophy, drama, religion, art and music once suggested man's capacity to be more noble, above his surface nature to conceive of a different reality. Politics was once also idealistic, looking for a path to build a better world. Like the film industry it is now purposely vapid to appeal to the lowest common denominator, which is most disturbingly expressed when Presidential candidates make stupid promises to a highly specific demographic to win by 10,000 votes in Pennsylvania, Florida and Ohio.

Politics is about winning, which is why science's entrée into leftist politics is so worrisome. This is what the Soviet Union did in an attempt to build a sustainable future, with a religious belief in science. Science shouldn't please the proletariat or voting blocks. It should seek objective, verifiable truth. As business interests corrupted politics, politics will corrupt science.

Politics is a streetfight. If both sides could get beyond that and debate ideas, I'd see an opening for solutions through political processes, but I don't see it happening for a long time, or until something really bad happens. But seriously, whichever Soros strategist decided that Nye and Tyson should be the face of leftist positions in the guise of science and the 97% of climate scientists agree on human pollution being the cause of climate change thing should be paid handsomely. (Was going to delete that last sentence, as I thought people wouldn't understand I was joking, I googled it as a lark and it happened to be true that Soros backed the Science March.) They basically won the battle before it was fought, even though Bill Nye clearly knows nothing about the climate.

Obviously, the 97% was a manipulation of data that people take wholesale, like one in five college students being raped and women making 78 cents on the dollar, or the one I caught the right making the other day that 51% of American Muslims believe in sharia, when it's probably only about half that number.

If I were still a Democrat, I wouldn't subscribe to the strategy of shaming that lost the presidency. Though in all seriousness the propaganda has worked. This is not because their strategy is better. It's because the left realized that they had the facts in their favor. They embellished instead of faking facts or turning the subjective into objective.

If you're a white man who denies climate change in New York or LA, you might as well be the evangelical demon exorcist and possible billionaire Pat Robertson. Across the country, you're only old and stupid if you deny climate change (I'm not sure how, but the left would probably claim his stance means he wants Honduran children to drown to death). Climate change denial is a shade worse than my pro patriotism and Judeo-Christian values stance that is called White Supremacist, even before I suggest that taking in Syrian refugees is not a great idea without a plan to reform Muslim extremism that is proven to work in the Middle East. Heavy vetting means nothing, especially when leftists indoctrinate moderate Muslims into hating the West with their multicultural ideology (one more clarification: You can be pro-diversity and be against multicultural ideology. I'm for multiculturalism's exact opposite position known as melting pot theory. Of course, we would need to build a culture that upholds values. These values were once the Constitution. I'm up for something else as long as we don't throw out the Constitution's authority in government).

As someone who takes on controversial stances, because I believe in them and not because I follow extreme Conservative doctrine, I don't deny climate change. This is not for fear of being branded an outcast. The theory makes sense. Who am I to argue? I hope I'm wrong, but I won't lie.

There seemed to be a clear correlation between carbon emissions and the rate of warming. Nevertheless, given how volatile our planet's climate is and how much we don't know about nature, including some pretty basic and fundamental questions about ecology, I am skeptical that anyone has any clear data or workable plan to solve this and I don't think abandoning cheap fossil fuels wholesale is possible or worth it. This is the only way many people in impoverished parts of the world make it to work or through the winter.

I also am extremely skeptical of climate scientists who have a lot to gain from climate change hysteria, made countless bad predictions in the past, like the earth is going to cool in the 70s. In 1989, The UN predicted countries would be wiped off the map. In 2005, the UN, predicted 50 million displaced people by 2010. The polar ice caps would melt by the Summer of 2013. Basically, the entire film, *An Inconvenient Truth* was wrong or hasn't happened yet.

The suppression of dissent is typical leftist tactics. It's just amazing that no one has branded them on the hysteria (probably for fear of appearing foolish) they have evoked about this so many times before and it's always under the auspices that things are different now.

While it's unlikely that a small minority of opinions is correct, especially when they largely agree with the establishment position, science is about the investigation all scenarios. Nothing would make me happier than seeing the MIT climatologist Richard Lindzen proving his skepticism to the UN. According to Dennis Prager, the video he made expressing the nonconformist climate change position was banned from public libraries. If he's right, this is like the Church and Galileo.

There is so much conflicting information in the world, making it doubly alarming that Trump's briefings come mostly in the form of Fox News with some occasional, "we call it *Deface the Nation*." God knows if that dog information at the top of the article was credible. It was in *The New York Times*, but what does that mean anymore? They were one of many institutions that barely reported on Assange's RT interview (that Hillary claims is part of why she lost) until after the election.

In our post-truth partisan world, people generally pick a side and accept the beliefs of those around them. Results of public policy matter to almost no one when judging a politician's decisions. When the electorate determine the policies we're in trouble.

Trump's campaign planned to keep America first, not agree to UN policies that may cost us a lot of money. Expanding the military budget, massive infrastructure (which I support) and the conflicts in Syria and North Korea are budgetary nightmares. Environmental policies are not massively expensive.

This is different. While it's sacrilege for me to acknowledge that Obama did anything right, there were a few things, including instilling confidence in America across the world and being trustworthy to the populace, even as he lied through his teeth. Not being able to directly benefit from say partnerships for loaning to alternative energy companies was stupid, as it was done without any financial incentive when we were in gargantuan debt and hobbling slowly out of a recession that nearly reached Depression status. Even though the federal government got fleeced, investing in companies like Tesla was good for the economy and the world.

Clean energy is thriving and will be one of the major industries of the future. Even if climate cooling occurs, people will probably not learn it from the mainstream media and will still buy those cars.

While the left is silencing dissenting views, they've abandoned unnecessary alarmist predictions. As much as it kills me, the left is taking the right approach on climate science. Even if the right-wingers are right and nothing happens in their lifetime, it's their job to shut up and do what can be done to evade potential disaster, even if it makes business more difficult, or goes against national self-interest. This is why it's idiotic to bring back coal mines to win a few votes in Pennsylvania and morally reprehensible. The successful indoctrination of believing in climate change or you're an idiot is actually a net positive, because the future is so uncertain. Nothing major could happen, but it's unpredictable. There is rather convincing evidence that something horrible could happen at almost any time. It will probably be something we've never seen before and have not properly prepared for.

In the age of neoliberalism, the main job of politicians is to manage peoples' perceptions. Obama was a master of that with the people with real influence. He was loved by those who didn't pay attention and those who did know George Bush was just as bad without doing generally sane things like pushing gay marriage through seven years after having to lie about not believing in it. The positive tone of the mainstream press, applauding Neville Chamberlain impressions in Syria and Iran, was enough to convince the Upper Middle-Class college educated non-intellectual nor ultra-leftist contingent of people who were genuinely proud of how they handled the first black president, to love Obama. They did this while agreeing with Clinton's characterization of working class poor Trump voters as deplorable racists.

The media and the elites view Trump as classless and crude. His hair and his inferiority complex are on the surface deplorable, as is the extent of the Russia collusion we know about (without getting into the BS conspiracies that drove MSNBC for months) and plans to use the presidency to give a boon to his own wealth that everyone sort of knows he greatly exaggerates.

Trump could employ every person in America at double the salary, broker peace in the Middle East and the elites would still be hounding him about Putin and "lies" which are almost always merely exaggerations of someone who wants the press to slaughter him for stupidity, so he can slam the press. This is because his supporters and all Republicans, even self-made 70-year-old millionaire Republicans already know that the media lies and when it doesn't lie its left bias is the most extreme it has been in their lifetime, even after Nixon. Though they are correct that the media lies, most of them find right wing media that also lies and reinforces their beliefs. Politics don't function properly.

We are critically divided. It can't get much worse. The people need to work together to build a better world. Politicians do everything badly. Everyone is being lied to and everyone is angry, even if it's hidden under the surface. This requires a change in perception as the world has been in decay for some time as technological revolutions that offered so much promise of a better world has mostly made everything worse.

The climate expresses exactly what is broken. We are on a path to destroy ourselves with our greed. We only have the ability to realize ourselves as individuals by doing the opposite of what we think is right. Being "true to ourselves" only divides us, because it balloons the ego making life unbearable. Very wealthy people have awakened a visceral rage inside them at the thought of Trump and it's ongoing. Whatever is bothering them is clearly not Trump. One who sees a flaw to the point of outrage is seeing a flaw in themselves. Clearly, it's easier to confront a buffoon on a television set who knows next to nothing about history and political process than to confront your own selfishness, especially when you purport to be a selfless liberal. We resent Trump (coastal elites like me and the very rich person described before), because we see ourselves in him, the power-hungry egomaniac that drives our worst actions. We only take care of ourselves and taking care of ourselves before we think of others is a slow death march. We feel it. That's why we use politics to feel morally superior in the first place.

There are no rational theories that will push us to a better hope. Our hope lies in an effort to connect to each other. A decision to love each other above our differences and let the force of love push us in the right direction. As long as we only look out for own interests, whether we're artists, philosophers, journalists, or multibillion dollar corporations, we will only draw further apart. As it stands now we live in a divided nation with no viable solutions. Some can handle the delusion, but it suffocates others, calling you from above to be human and feel the heart of another person you have no natural desire to know or understand. It will open up thoughts and dreams like nothing you've ever experienced on a VR headset.

MILO YIANNOPOULOS: FREE SPEECH ADOCATE OR FASCIST?

Depending on which party you support, it is likely you already know the answer to the title question. The Hillary campaign website painted him as the leader of a White Supremacist group called the alt-right, simplifying a complex political movement that mostly derides white supremacists. Every mainstream media (liberal) reporter is filled with something between fake and visceral outrage when they mention his name or interview him. He like fellow Trump supporter Azealia Banks was banned by twitter for supporting Trump, though officially for trafficking hate speech. Trump supporters with the exception of real neo-Nazis and the Christian Right love him.

If one were to take the things British provocateur Milo Yiannopoulos says at face value it would be hard to take him seriously. What shocks me much more than his antics, is that the liberal lamestream media and politically correct millennials seem to believe he is a modern-day fascist militant, when I take his act about as seriously as Andy Kaufman wrestling women.

That said, Milo definitely has a certain charisma. He's sort of like the gay best friend in a 90s' romantic comedy, but one who uses his catty power to take down feminists and the liberal establishment without shying away from the gritty details of his sexual escapades in nasty language. Though he's on the wrong side on a bunch of issues, I can't help but admire the way he shatters stereotypes and makes no sense to the left.

Like early Howard Stern or 80s' Eddie Murphy stand up (way better acts than Milo that if made today would have casted them as fascists), you can't help but want to see what he'll say next.

His talent is provocation and there's no easier or funnier group to provoke than oversensitive millennials. When he mouths off on Muslims, feminists and Black Lives Matter activists it stirs real tension. It's a shocking sight in our anaesthetized culture PC culture.

Idealist millennials are "triggered" by what campuses define as his "hate speech," that some have ridiculously argued is more powerful than actual violence. For inciting protests and building a massive following of alt right trolls whose memes played a role in electing "Daddy" (the creepily affectionate nickname he gave our president), to the left he became a "Dangerous Faggot," exactly what he intended when he named his tour that.

Though he spends an inordinate amount of time extolling the virtues of sleeping with many black men for a serious political commentator ("If you spent time in my bedroom, you'd know I'm not a white Supremacist"), he's not a complete buffoon, though as rival ex Breitbart editor at large Ben Shapiro notes, "he's not nearly as intelligent as his British accent makes him appear."

Still, when Milo spouts out vitriolic facts, very pleased with himself (lazily, usually the same facts he repeats every time he addresses the media), to 19-year-old girls asking "Did you know that feminism is the belief that men and women are equal?" on a big stage he looks like an intellectual titan.

Milo is clearly a compelling figure. In spite of this, there's no logical explanation for the fury of outrage he stirs in people. Though he loves the teenagers sending Nazi propaganda on Facebook with their red hats, he's a half-Greek half-Jewish homosexual that at least publicly condemns racism. He's a bully on a mission to poke fun at the hypersensitive liberal society his audience have either submitted to or taken a part in constructing. Like Madonna and The Sex Pistols (who he compares himself to but seems to think were around in the 90s), he has shaken Western culture at its core and the left are playing into the palm of his hand.

Once one of many niche conservative dudes on the internet shouting about Colin Kaepernick, the absurdity of feminism, racism against whites and the "conspiracy organization" Black Lives Matter, he has risen to national prominence because of the clearly unjust response he is getting from protestors. These protestors, who are likely funded by a liberal billionaire disrupter named George Soros, make him a household name and a bestselling author.

The failure of the left to see the irony in calling Milo a fascist, while burning his books is not lost on Trump supporters. It also gives him a huge platform to show how hypocritical liberals are. This is precisely the reason Trump won in the first place. The liberal establishment is very successfully building a world where the accepted norms of culture prevent the acceptance of alternative opinions. Most of the left would be happy if America did what Sweden did, making it illegal to criticize taking in refugees and Islam.

While Bill Maher shouts about how awesome it is that the

democrats have their own tea party, to traditional White Middle-Class Democrats who voted for Trump in Ohio and Pennsylvania, the new liberals who smash buildings and befriend jihadist sympathizers with anarchist affiliations is a hell of a lot worse than Trump making a mockery of the media that they know like the Clintons is beholden to corporate interests. George Soros, in his infinite stupidity, is ensuring Trump will be reelected.

The problem with Milo for the left is that he's not wrong about everything. He understands that the establishment is becoming oppressive. He has facts to fight the unfounded blind belief that every progressive initiative is improving the world. He is converting liberals to the side that the institutions are deathly afraid of.

The press, the universities and the liberal establishment is befuddled. Even old-school Republican neoconservatives are calling intellectuals in the president's administration Nazis. The neoconservatives and the liberals (the elites, think both Clintons, both Bushes and Alan Greenspan) have been peddling such nonsense for so long they have no idea how to react to someone who obfuscates the readily available "inarguable truth." Milo Yiannopoulos, like Trump, is just the reaction to a hypocritical system.

The politicians are angry, because they use to have to pretend to be truthful and virtuous with a complicit press that sometimes asks hard questions, but as is clear to Trump supporters, this was all in service of the illusion of objectivity and checks and balances. Everyone knew the politicians were lying, but no one really cared. This is why most of the right don't care that Trump lies about objective truth.

Trump supporters willfully dismiss the monoculture of absolutist political correctness and intolerance of alternative perspectives that has been the rule of thumb for decades. They understand what the intellectual Trump senior national security official Michael Anton noted under a pseudonym before the election, "For two generations at least, the Left has been calling everyone to their right Nazis." Milo said the same of anyone to the right of Jane Fonda.

This you're either with us or you're a Nazi strategy has maintained the status quo, distracting us from right-wing military policies of destroying dictatorships that ultimately lead to the rise of Muslim theocracies and chaos. The problem is that in today's world the hypocrisy is so blatant it ensures Trump will maintain his power. While people like Milo convert people to his side regularly, the left needs to find a better antidote to this than millennial snowflakes crying about micro-aggression, while burning things and destroying property.

A RELUCTANT MILLENNIAL TACKLES THE MILLENNIAL PROBLEM

No one wants to be a Millennial, except for a few weird undergrads who write politically correct versions of dictionaries that offer *simple* alternative wordings for offensive phrases like "poor person" such as "person who lacks advantages that others have, low economic status related to a person's education, occupation and income." This, and a myriad of other reasons, is why Millennial became a dirty word like hipster or cis-gendered male.

When I speak of Millennials, I mostly mean what the media portrays them as, Middle to Upper Class students and graduates of somewhat to highly prestigious universities and colleges. This infectious species that polices the appropriateness of Halloween costumes and takes off weeks from school to cope with the election of a person who doesn't share their values in "safe spaces" chockfull of art and dog therapy.

While I'm broadly a liberal, I'm perturbed by the Millennial snowflake reaction to Trump's election that ignores the massive expansion of neoliberalism, warmongering, creation of the Syrian conflict, and pissed on civil liberties under the last administration. This blind acceptance of the Democratic party by college students is just one example of how this segment of the population constructs a protective shell that makes them ignorant of the world, and unable to function in the world when they graduate. At the very age when one would expect people to form cogent political positions, self-absorption or laziness seems to prevent Millennials from keeping informed. They rely on appearances above reliable information.

Just like the Millennial snowflake generation is ill-prepared to debate politics rationally, they are ill-equipped for the challenges of adult life. They cannot tolerate unfairness, are still shocked by ubiquitous hypocrisy other than their own and don't understand their voice doesn't necessarily matter. After being coddled by their parents and their universities, young people enter the job market with the expectation of a fair world where everything is taken care of for them. All the while, the pleasure centers in their brains are corrupted by social media and technology that gives validation in the form of likes and right swipes. Combined with the fact that most Millennials have the ability to distract themselves with every film, funny clip, porno clip, show, song and album ever made in minutes, it's not hard to see why my generation lacks motivation.

A video describing the workplace entitlement of Millennials by Simon Sinek has 140 million views and counting, with an additional four million views on YouTube. He describes that after leaving schools that protect Millennials in safe spaces, these young people find themselves in a fractured dog eat dog world. They were failed by the excessive praise of their parents, the participation trophies that "devalues the reward for those who actually work hard."

Even as employers go to great lengths to coddle this mass of snowflakes, they are still ineffective and depressed, with lower self-esteem than any generation in recent history. The cost of this is sure to be devastating to American society. Young adults are forced to lean on their parents when they come to find they have no ability to take care of themselves. Most overcome the trauma of this disappointment, but many do not.

When the snowflakes come to an understanding that the world owes them nothing, in a marginally improving job market, they break down. They can't consider contrary opinions, let alone the voices of superiors that criticize their work. While they overwhelmingly search for work that impacts the world positively, personally wide swaths of Millennials have found no meaning to their existence, where they are unable to appreciate what they have, often because they understand deep down that they don't really deserve it in the first place.

One of my literary heroes, Bret Easton Ellis, famously dubbed Millennials as "Generation Wuss," acknowledging the generational divide between him as a 50-year-old and his boyfriend who is roughly my age. He notes their reactions to his provocations on Twitter by saying, "My huge generalities touch on their over-sensitivity, their insistence that they are right despite the overwhelming proof that suggests they are not, their lack of placing things within context, the overreacting, the passive-aggressive positivity, and, of course, all of this exacerbated by the meds they've been fed since childhood by over-protective "helicopter" parents mapping their every move." The irony is altogether lost on them when their oversensitivity blossoms in the face of Ellis' critiques of Millennial oversensitivity.

Rather than acknowledge something is wrong with their worldview, I see the snowflakes drown out all voices that don't conform to their politically correct secular "everyone is special" belief system. When I harmlessly posted a satire Onion style piece entitled, "Hamas Endorses Sanders for President, Calls Him "Jew We Can Believe In"," a Millennial threatened to block me on Facebook. Though this isn't exclusively a problem with Millennials, the Trump supporters I know can tell you much worse stories of losing contact with people they were once close to of all ages.

The sad reality is that Millennials who profess to care for the less fortunate are largely a generation of narcissists, who are too precious to encounter anything they disagree with, however poorly researched and formed their own views are. They profess to want to help Haiti, Syria and the Sudan, while obsessing over their petty problems to a degree that makes them incapable of considering another person's plight.

A few years ago, Narcissistic Personality Disorder was removed from the psychiatric disorder manual known as the DSM, one could argue largely because the traits were too prevalent. Unlike the DSM, it is my belief we need to diagnose the sickness of narcissism that ails society and work together to create a world that values and rewards hard work, accomplishment and selflessness.

In a time when people gravitate towards protected bubbles, entitled Millennials desperately need to connect with a diversity of values and opinions. Even the Millennial Messiah, Obama, said as much in his farewell address, but will this generation listen? To gather the strength to tackle the challenges the Baby Boomer and early Gen X generation of parents caused the Millennials with overpraise and helicopter parenting, a young person with intentions of success needs to decide to want to care about others, (This may shock some snowflakes) including the people with different beliefs and values. Essentially, Millennials need to learn to become human beings. How can a young person grow and mold his or her self without considering different views?

We will never be able to face the huge political divisions and the Millennial problem without truly learning lessons from the past. Though I don't agree with a lot of what Obama has done, I share his romanticism about America. When he says in his farewell speech, "What a radical idea, the great gift that our Founders gave to us. The freedom to chase our individual dreams through our sweat, and toil, and imagination—and the imperative to strive together as well, to achieve a common good, a greater good," it angers me that our country is doing nothing of the sort.

It's not hard to see why "Make America Great Again" appealed to nearly half of the American population, who are fed up with the political correctness of the left invoked most laughably by young people. If Millennials wish to both thrive as individuals and unite for the common good, it begins with connecting with and caring about other Americans, to break through the narcissistic shell. This can only begin through listening and striving to understand the largely not evil people who elected our president.

You may be wondering why a 29-year-old sounds so much like a middle-aged man. For the jaded few who recognized the writer of this article doth protest too much, there is a real reason. As a spoiled, overpraised Millennial, who put a lot of stock in my high IQ, with a history of drug and alcohol abuse, I was wired like a ticking time bomb. Like all the great Millennials, I had a rather large ego and very little self-confidence, a piss poor work ethic, and simultaneous fears of both success and failure. My first book, *The Egotist*, outlines the extent of my self-destructive narcissistic tendencies and how I overcame them by developing empathy for others and overcoming my fears by letting go of my Millennial victim mentality.

In spite of my progress, I still routinely blast opinions that contradict my own, procrastinate, take valid criticism like the claws of a bear and blame others for my flaws and failures. The big difference is that by connecting to others who I am not naturally drawn to, with the intention of caring for others above benefitting myself, I have the ability to transform my ego into something that can help other people. I can lose myself. I feel connected to the hearts of others above their minds, appearances and opinions. When others attempt to do the same, this collective desire leads us to a place of truth, warmth and connection. In spite of my self-destructive wiring, these experiences teach me to thrive through routine and extraordinary stress, as well as traumas that in the past would have destroyed me. Since I understand the pain of post-grad Millennial life, I greatly sympathize with the plight of growing up in a broken environment and the lost feeling one has when they're unsure of how to make their way in the world. Having overcome a lot of these overly prevalent faulty traits, I urge Millennials to try and lose themselves in real connections with others who think differently than they do, face to face, away from the screens that have a tendency to drive us apart.

CAN WE SAVE THE WORLD?

Even though we are keenly aware that human beings are destroying the world, rather than dwell on this fact, we distract ourselves to avoid confronting this reality. As someone deeply invested in Kabbalah study and a movement aspiring to bring about social change, I still find myself drowning in the huge and instantly accessible abyss of fair to excellent TV shows popping out with alacrity. Rather than do something about this clear crisis of the human spirit (profit motivated corporations are destroying our natural resources, a completely dysfunctional political system, antibiotics are becoming less successful at doing their jobs, the gap between the rich and poor in even the most developed countries is unsustainable, the rise of Islamic extremists, drug addiction on the rise), I'm often satiated by acknowledging these problems exist by the middle brow and upper middle brow television I consume. I think this is the pattern many people are stuck in. Too busy to try and improve the world, I like many people am entertained by the very real phenomena that the art tackles. While the systemic failure of America and global society makes for good art, isn't this clear imbalance supposed to enrage the populous?

On my Tumblr page, I've recently compiled all the film and television I've been watching. It has made me contemplate the sad reality of our existence. In these fictional worlds, everyone seems to have a desire for more, and if not more, for things to come together in a way that life won't allow for. Then in the real world, there are constant signs I see of society decaying. First there was the much too long flirtation with the conman Donald Trump as being a viable candidate for the presidency. The VMAs are awarding criminally bad artists who only seem to be interested in legalizing and enjoying marijuana, while they sell the dream that everyone is valuable and worthy and should dream big, while they orbit in highly exclusive cliques that their adoring fans would do anything to spend a night with. On the VMAs, the corporate speak of politically correct brainwashed ideologies are permeating throughout even the supposedly sordid elements of popular society (Miley Cyrus, Kanye West). Everyone feels good about themselves (their positive messages) in order to ignore confronting reality dead on, or to distract themselves from the pain society creates as it is currently constructed.

In mass culture, we don't in any meaningful way address the failure of the system. We don't look for alternatives. This is what is so surprising and refreshing about *Mr. Robot*. Aside from it being the most addictive show I've seen in years, I am shaken by its drama being centered upon acknowledging the world is a huge mess in need of an ideological revolution. And it doesn't take place in some dystopian future. It takes place in a heightened version of New York City today. The hero of the show is a morphine addicted hacker, who winds up being swept into the orbit of a group of hackers who wish to wipe out the credit card debt records and create chaos to empower the people to create a new economic system, where the 1 percent no longer feeds on the misfortune of the weak. The idea is so revolutionary, so un-American, you would think this would cause some sort of uproar, but it doesn't. We see that the world is in a state of crisis so undeniable that we can build drama to this effect with few questions being asked. However, we don't see its viewers banding together to destroy the institutions that created this world. Instead, we enjoy this drama based on a reality we are all too aware of. I came late to the party and took in 10 episodes in a few days.

In order to avert global catastrophe there needs to be a full-scale change in human values. In today's world, we measure ourselves by the fulfillment of our ego, which for most of us comes in the size of our bank accounts, or the praise we receive from our accomplishments. We do this instead of looking to do our part to reform the nature of society. The current economic model is based on human nature, our will to receive. Human desire leads all people to seek pleasure for themselves at the expense of all other calculations. If someone is charitable, it is only because he or she derives pleasure from helping others. His or her ego is satiated by the acknowledgement they are doing good for other people, but they are still looking out for themselves. In order for society to truly reform, we would consciously need to try and fulfill the desires of others above our own. We would need to work against our nature. By seeing ourselves as a means of improving each other's lives and only looking out for our own necessities (not just eating bread and water like monks, everyone is different and would have their own calculations to make) we would receive infinite fulfillment, because we would not be burdened by our desire for more pleasure.

You may be thinking it would be impossible for society to change such a deeply embedded value system and your assertion would make a lot of sense. However, I would argue, I see values changing all the time, and faster than ever. Fifty years ago, it would be unthinkable to tell a parent to not beat his child. 10 years ago, gay marriage and the legalization of marijuana were such unthinkable positions no mainstream political candidate in their right mind would mention them. In our deeply interconnected world, all it takes is a minority of 10 percent to hold an unshakable belief to change the majority opinion. If people could establish small societies that worked by these values, their example would influence the world. As humans, it is our responsibility to try and improve our world, and a revolution in our consciousness—a decision to redefine the meaning of happiness and success—is the place to start.

THE HEALING POWER OF CONNECTION

Johann Hari nearly broke the Internet last week with his article, "The Likely Cause of Addiction Has Been Discovered, and It Is Not What You Think." In his article he argues that the cause of addiction is not the drugs themselves, but the addict's inability to connect with others as a byproduct of the environment he or she inhabits. He shares some really compelling evidence supporting his point. Nearly everyone who breaks his or her hip is given diamorphine (pharmaceutical heroin) over extended periods and virtually no one gets addicted to the substance. Further, even rats, who alone in a cage, famously will kill themselves with heroin *en lieu* of food, won't necessarily become addicted to drugs that are freely introduced in "Rat Park," a communal rat paradise that was built to conduct an experiment. Maybe more interesting to addicts, when addicted rats are taken out of isolation and into "Rat Park," a rat paradise with lots of friends, the majority of them recover from their addiction relatively painlessly. Hari argues that the reason for this is because animals and human beings are wired toward bonding with others and forming connections. Absent of this connection they turn to drugs.

While this article certainly didn't shock me as an addict—I had needed to change my environment to aid in my recovery—if it weren't for what I learned in recovery, it would have brought up more questions in my mind than answers. If all we need to recover is human connection, why is it so difficult for addicts to recover? How can we shape a better world where connection is the norm? Would this world eradicate the plague of addiction? Looking at the comments section of the article, I could feel the frustration of people who were close to addicts who did everything they could to love and support the addicts in their life, only to find them dead or unappreciated—people who opened their homes to relatives, only to be stolen from and lied to. What are we doing right as a society and what are we doing wrong?

As Thomas Pynchon attests in *Inherent Vice*, "As long as American life was something to be escaped from, the cartel would always be assured a bottomless pool of new customers." If we are going to eradicate addiction, we need society as a whole to be a "Rat Park" geared towards human connection.

But what is stopping us from creating a world where connection thrives over addiction? I have rarely heard people argue that human connection is a bad thing, but something prevents us from taking steps towards achieving this state. In our materialistic, ego-driven culture, our nature is to resist anything that doesn't clearly benefit us as individuals. Many addicts have made the calculation that taking a drug is less painful than trying to love others. If support doesn't help them, how can we help addicts out of this cycle of pain?

When we look at nature, we see a vast interconnected system where everything is dependent on everything else. When we look at humanity, for the most part we see individuals working for their own benefit. We see competition that destroys human bonding and love. All of us and especially addicts need to reform to care for others above our selfish wiring.

My book, *The Egotist*, tells the story of how I as a hopeless drug addict found an environment in Israel founded on the principles of better human connection, and introducing a plan for correcting the nature of humanity towards better social cohesion. I try to express how connecting with human beings gave me answers to questions I never would have known to ask and transformed me from a selfish addict to someone who tries to devote his life to the wellbeing of others. I want others to understand that working to help others in need is endlessly fulfilling, while working solely for myself was a dead end I needed to escape. If we are able to annul our ego to understand and care for others above our own problems and burdensome resentments we will possess the tools to rid our society of the addiction crisis that almost certainly threatens to kill someone close to you.

ADDICTS HOLD UP A MIRROR TO SOCIETY

I've spent thousands of hours working on my recovery and have read all of the AA approved materials multiple times. I also turned to the media. I listened to Dr. Drew's Loveline and watched Celebrity Rehab, and read many memoirs and novels on the subject of addiction. What I can't get out of my head is how much Johann Hari really offered a new perspective with *Chasing the Scream* and how he succeeded in convincing us that our entire attitude to this issue is wrong. I had heard glimpses of his perspective in the novels of Thomas Pynchon and in the recovery rooms, but this vital point of view was entirely absent from the broad mainstream media. People were unaware of the truth about addiction and this is precisely why the now infamous article was read by millions and shared by 260K people on Facebook.

The war in drugs is exactly what it sounds like. It is a persecution of the substances themselves. American policy believed that if only we could get rid of these drugs and take down the cartels there would be no more drug addiction. But what if the drugs are merely a symptom of a bigger void that lives in the mind of an addict? What if addiction is really only a lack of connection to other people and an inability to feel meaning in life? This is exactly what Hari proposes.

Even before I turned to drugs, I was obsessed with addiction.

First, as a six-year-old child when my Gen-X heroes all mourned the suicide of Kurt Cobain and now as someone who has felt the terror of needing substances just to get through the day, and has seen my peers overdose and kill themselves. I am fascinated by the minds of addicts. They are the type of people who seem to be eternally dissatisfied with life. Even after seeing the death toll of addiction, a part of me still has a romantic attachment to them. As a child, I wanted to know what makes them click and why so many of them are so talented. I was always drawn to them. I immediately connected with their warped sensibility. Even then a part of me knew I was one of them. I was searching for something they knew. They seemed to possess a truth that was blind to the average Joe 9-5ers and these drug addicted artists made bold steps to shroud the conformity of daily life I always resented.

The addict is an expression of the true state of the world. A world where people are entirely evil, motivated entirely by their own self-interest, even when this interest comes in the guise of helping others. Everyone is a slave to the way they feel. Addicts are just people with a quick remedy to their uncomfortable feelings. Their brain has been reprogrammed to be unable to tolerate discomfort. The discomfort everyone feels from time to time. When people are connected and feel a sense of purpose, they do not turn to drugs. This is why, as Hari writes, 85% of Vietnam veterans were able to quit the drug after coming home from the war. They had a family and friends to support them. Their environment wasn't pushing drugs on them once they came home. Maybe as Alva Noe asserts in her reflection on Hari's article, "The Fight Against Addiction: Is Love All You Need?," they weren't really addicts. An addict is someone who internally is in a state of isolation, whether they are alone or hosting a party. The addict is in tune with the ways of reality--their evil nature. But this romantic attachment is why addicts hurt so many people. We are attracted to self-seeking behavior and danger.

However, these tragic figures do much more harm than good. We need to find ways to help them, if only so they can stop hurting us. When we look at the people who could stop using heroin with almost no trouble, we have to ask ourselves, as Americans and as citizens of the world, why does the sore of addiction continue to grow? Why do 22 million people suffer from addiction? Why do we allow addiction to hurt 100 million relatives of these 22 million? What is it about the society we live in that encourages isolation over connection? The only means the world has of helping these people is to reform the environment people inhabit and that means we as a world need to be nourished by new values. Only with the awareness that we are unconsciously harming others merely by existing will we be able to come to new, better solutions for all the problems that ail the world.

What Hari beautifully illustrates in his book and in his article, is that we are slaves to our environment. He does this simply, by expressing that rats in isolation will almost certainly kill themselves when they are given drugs, while rats in "Rat Park," a communal rat paradise will use drugs casually without becoming dependent on them. We see a good environment instills positive values. The danger of this is that an unhealthy environment will do more harm than good.

America is clearly in a state of decline. Though the economy has recovered substantially in the last few years and we see small improvements from time to time, nearly every facet of society has been corrupted by our egos. We all have the undying belief that we are as they say in the rooms of recovery terminally unique. This uniqueness and entitlement that we all once believed would build a better world has proven to be a drain on the lives of ordinary people. This is because, as I wrote in my book, *The Egotist*:

"The world seems to mirror Ayn Rand's philosophy of the individual that says, 'The mind is an attribute of the individual. There is no such thing as a collective brain. There is no such thing as a collective thought. An agreement reached by a group of men is only a compromise or an average drawn upon many individual thoughts. It is a secondary consequence.'"

"It has become clear equal opportunity is an illusion. Upward mobility has all but vanished from society. Society's progress is being hampered because the people who hold the levers of power, those with the money, live in a self-constructed environment where this idea of the supremacy of the individual dominates, to the detriment of everyone else."

We have reached the limits of such a system and though I know that communism and even socialism will not solve any of these problems, we need to begin to work in a way where we care for others in order to care for the entire society. These ideas don't need to be confined to support groups, where there is an awareness that the ego corrupts absolutely. When man and governments will hold the self-evident truth that man must work against his nature to be good to others, we will be able to construct a much stronger, more unified society by searching for mutually beneficial solutions. We will be able to transcend our nature.

POLITICAL CORRECTNESS

(Source, Wikipedia Commons)

You can't watch television these days without hearing people talk about political correctness. The term is constantly used and misused to many ends. Donald Trump's campaign revels in the idea of a need to be rid of political correctness and not-so-subtly proposes that this concept is destroying America. His message is clear. If we want to make America great again, we need to ignore the liberal agenda that bars us from offending anyone and ignores the truth. According to Trump, political correctness is the reason why people no longer speak their minds and is to blame for the surge of Mexican immigrants destroying America. The danger of this refreshing idea that we need to stop being politically correct is it became a kind of code-speak for racism and bullying. Trump claimed that Mexican immigrants were criminals and rapists, that John McCain wasn't a hero because he was captured, and compared <u>Ben Carson's temper</u> (also a champion of political incorrectness) to child molestation. However inane and unfounded in fact Trump is, his blatant disregard of political correctness is a large part of his popularity that has lasted much longer than any reasonable person would have assumed was possible some months back.

But Trump is for the crazies and the naïve. I still believe if he goes against Hillary in the general election, it'll be the most devastating blow to the Republican party, since Watergate, if not ever. Most of the semi-rational minds in his party agree with this assessment. In spite of this, Trump has locked onto two key ideas are that are too powerful to ignore. Firstly, that the government is bought and sold by corporations and secondly, that political correctness is a cancer on the heart of America and the modern world. When I speak of political correctness, I don't believe in blaming Mexican immigrants for the decline in American greatness, or the right to call women pigs judged solely by the merits of their bone structure, but I do believe political correctness is making honest discourse more and more difficult, if not impossible.

When I began thinking about how I would address this topic, I wanted to relate Trump to the sentimental narratives in the culture that the older white male demographic was fed up with. Things that I agree and disagree with to varying degrees, like the new ideal that there needs to be a term called cis gender to relate to the 99.7% of the population that is not transgender and whether, or whether or not it is racist to place minority actors in subordinate roles to white characters (taxi drivers, maids, etc.) in television and film. I wanted to explore whether Effie, the producer on *Project*

Greenlight, was crazy for freaking out about a black man cast as a limo driver in the very bad movie they were producing. Then I wanted to counterbalance that point with Aziz Ansari's brilliantly funny, ideologically sound depiction of a childhood where all the Indian characters were racist caricatures on *Master of None.* How could we find the balance in society without limiting the freedom of the artists making the movies?

I was interested in the ridiculous notion that movies should not be judged on their aesthetic merits, but on their ideological aims. Specifically, I wanted to tackle why the internet was aghast at Quentin Tarantino when he said in an interview profile by Bret Easton Ellis that *Selma* should have won an Emmy, comparing the Martin Luther King biopic to a TV movie, and compare that to the fury aimed at Francine Prose sixteen years ago for making the "shocking" statement that Maya Angelou's heavily metaphor-laden prose was bad writing. And then came Paris.

In the grand scheme of things, does anyone really care that self-important filmmakers usually win awards over better filmmakers? It no longer felt all that important to discuss the aesthetic merits of a few heavily lauded minority writers and filmmakers (some good and some bad). I know that it's not racist to have aesthetic problems with *12 Years a Slave* or *Schindler's List* (or any film for that matter), because I look at films in a nuanced way the general population doesn't care to. I know it is un-American to not let someone have a poor opinion about a movie tackling social issues. Then I came to the conclusion that the very levers that make it racist to criticize a fairly good movie about Martin Luther King also are to blame for the fact it is considered racist by some to criticize Europe opening its doors to 60,000,000 refugees.

I know that social progress comes with some speed bumps, as

people navigate the politically correct means of delivering messages. One day you can say something one way and the next, only a drunk uncle at Thanksgiving dinner can say it. I get it. America has a long history of racism, sexism and has been fairly horrible to most if not all minorities at some time or another and this horrifyingly continues to this day in spite of the best intentions of the majority of Americans. In our attempt to improve this undignified treatment of everyone excepting white males with money in their pockets, we need to alter language to ensure we don't hurt each other quite as much. For the most part this is a good thing. The problem with political correctness is that it tends to ignore nuance and truth in the service of not hurting feelings.

Generally, these little hiccups that disallow opinions are not so important. The problem with political correctness broadly is that people cannot criticize anything or anyone in a disadvantaged situation, for fear of going against the corporatized politically correct narrative. Sometimes when I defend Israel, I feel like I'm living in *1984*. This is part of the reason Israel gets blamed for everything going on in Gaza, instead of Hamas and the other neighboring Arab nations, and it is entirely the reason that the backward Fundamentalist Muslim beliefs of hundreds of millions of the nearly two billion Muslims in the world get a free pass. We have been conditioned to believe that criticizing anything to do with a minority is fundamentally wrong. The "forward-thinking" people have also been trained to believe that any idea coming from the right is entirely wrong. Again, a lack of nuance.

As a child of the 90s, I was indoctrinated with political correctness from an early age. One day in third grade, we were led into an assembly where we heard the thoughts of a well-meaning person, an Upper Middle Class white woman explaining prejudice to my mostly-white Upper Middle-Class Connecticut elementary school. We heard the woman consider what it was to be politically correct and why it was necessary not to call black people black. Instead, we were supposed to say African American. We were told discrimination was wrong. Towards the end, she kind of lost track of her argument and went on a soliloquy about judgment. How we should be prejudiced in our decision-making. That it was necessary to prejudge things from our experience. She gave the example of buying a car and not buying an English car because the prejudiced opinion was that those cars often had engine failure and a boatload of others problems. However, we should not make the same judgments about people.

In spite of all a lot of the other nonsense she was spewing, she was right. Individuals should always be given the benefit of the doubt. It is patently wrong to prejudge them. However, it is not patently wrong to examine the ideologies that influence these people. When we look at Paris, we should remember that Fundamentalist Islam is responsible for the Charlie Hebdo attack last year and 129 more deaths last week. We can't blindly follow the liberal agenda that it was a heroic act to allow tens of millions of Muslims, many of whom have been infected with Fundamentalist ideology, into Europe and expect everything to run smoothly. We cannot let our well-meaning liberal intentions confuse us into blindly accepting cultures that oppress people and endanger the freedoms we fought so hard to attain and are still fighting for. As much as I would like to help those being oppressed by ISIS, if we do not look at the world realistically for fear of offending people, what values of freedom will we be fighting for?

JEWISH AMERICAN LITERATURE: A STORY OF IMPOSSIBLE ASSIMILATION

Multiculturalism is a means of teaching children about themselves by exploring different cultures, whether these cultures are foreign to them, or their own. While I am not of the mind we have nothing to learn from the model of essentialism, where we learn about the nature of the world from the perspective of the classics (mostly dead white men), there is a richness to culture and human experience that cannot be tackled exclusively by Plato and William Shakespeare. Further, people don't read as much. This is precisely why multiculturalism has become so essential as of late. The way to make students understand and learn to love literature is to relate reading to their own lives (though I wish it didn't have to) and to offer a glimpse into other worlds.

Multiculturalism is a method for both. An African American student may have an innate interest in African American culture, but he or she may also want to know what it's like to grow up in China. While the environment a Chinese boy living on a farm inhabits may be entirely foreign to an African American student living in Brooklyn, a unit exploring these differences will ultimately highlight our similarities more than our differences. Literature is a means of understanding what it is to be human and teaches us to sympathize with each other above our differences.

One culture that is often left out of curriculums on multiculturalism is Jewish culture. While most curriculums do something that recognizes the Holocaust, a particularly relevant culture to students, especially New Yorkers, is Jewish American life. Jewish assimilation was a very slow and painful process in America. Though American Jews were eventually welcomed into the forefront of American culture, the path was met with a lot of resistance and Jewish authors reveal both a desire for Jews to be part of the culture at large and an uneasy connection to their past.

Interestingly, there were very few notable Jewish American authors at the beginning of the 20th century. Anti-Semitism was more or less a rule of thumb in American life and there was a lot of distrust of Jews, just as there was distrust of all the immigrants. As Christopher Hitchens wrote in his book on Saul Bellow, "Remember that when Bellow was growing up, Lionel Trilling could be sacked from a teaching post at Columbia on the grounds that a Jew could not really appreciate English literature."

This is precisely why, arguably the first great Jewish American author Nathaniel West, an atheist and son of Russian Jewish immigrants, changed his name from Nathan Weinstein and wrote exclusively about characters who weren't Jewish. Like the Hollywood directors and actors of Jewish descent, he hid his Judaism to be accepted by American culture. He masked who he was, so he could be an author rather than a "Jewish author" before his tragic death, making one wonder what direction his work would have gone if he hadn't been killed in automobile accident at the age of thirty-seven.

Would he have confronted his uneasy relationship with his faith more directly? While his contemporaries, like F. Scott Fitzgerald and Ernest Hemingway, were interested in Jewish characters, they were often portrayed with a lot of contempt. The stereotypes about Jews were on full display (note the conniving boxer and untalented Robert Cohn in *The Sun Also Rises*, and the tooth cufflinked caricature of Meyer Lansky named Meyer Wolfshiem in *The Great Gatsby*). The widespread prevalence of anti-Semitism in American culture was particularly prevalent in the snobbery of literary world, until so many Jewish authors achieved inarguable greatness. If you look at the Jewish integration to American life, they were essentially unwanted and because of a desire to succeed, they forced their way into to the top of every sphere of American life.

In the next generation of authors, most notably in the 50s and 60s, Jewish authors began to write specifically from the perspective of Jewish characters, often boldly confronting these stereotypes head on and like a bullet. You cannot really begin to look at this period without mentioning Jewish authors. There was Arthur Miller, Saul Bellow, Philip Roth, Isaac Asimov, Alan Ginsberg, Bernard Malamud to name a few, and the trashy but ideologically brilliant *Exodus*, telling the story of Israeli independence was the bestselling book since *Gone With the Wind*.

Jewish exceptionalism in the field of letters is maybe why Jewish literature isn't often contained in the study and curriculums of multicultural literature. However, it would be unwise not to tackle Jewish American writing, especially in New York City, where twenty percent of the population is Jewish, because anti-Semitism is steeply on the rise as of late and there is still a constant feud between Jewish traditionalism and secular society. Not only do these works have considerable merit, but also, they ask questions that are still relevant today. While Jews are no longer viewed as separate from the mainstream American life and Jews are present in all spheres of American society, it is worth examining what it means to be Jewish, the controversial subject of Israel and the persistence of anti-Semitism in the world today.

Philip Roth's story "Eli the Fanatic," is a prime example of a work specifically concerning Jewish assimilation. Unlike most Jewish American literature and most of Roth's work, it is a story mainly about religious Jews. The main conflict in the story is the emergence of religious Jews in a residential area. Leo Tzuref, a German Rabbi, starts a yeshiva in his home, in a New York City suburb. A yeshiva is a Jewish tradition where kids, usually teenagers live together in a home and study Torah. Due to a technicality, the townspeople try and get Tzuref to leave, by offering the legal reason that it is illegal to start a boarding school in a residential area. Very quickly we see that the problem is not one of zoning, but the feeling that the presence of 18 Orthodox Jewish students will adversely affect the community.

Ted, the leader of the purge of the Jews makes no qualms about expressing his disdain for the town's new inhabitants. "Goddam fanatics," Ted said. "This is the 20th century, Eli. Now it's the guy with the hat. Pretty soon all the little Yeshivah boys'll be spilling down into town." "Next thing they'll be after our daughters." The town sees Tzuref as a threat to the community of Woodenton, because he is instilling old world Jewish values into the modern American suburb. It is a prime example of xenophobia that can be related to every race and nationality in American suburbs. Some cultures chose to be ghettoized, while others did their best to be American in thought. Jews chose both paths to an extreme degree, which is why there are still big Orthodox communities that do their best to remain separate from the societies they inhabit and why Rachel Silberstein noted in her article "Can You Be an Atheist and a Jew at the Same Time? David Silverman Says No" that "60 percent of American Jews believe that Judaism is mainly a matter

of ancestry, culture, and values, rather than of
religious observance."

As the story progresses, we see that this xenophobia quickly
develops into clear anti-Semitism. What starts as a discomfort with
the funny Baal Shem Tov hats the Orthodox Jews wear, becomes
a discomfort with fanatical religion. "We're not just dealing with
people—these are religious fanatics is what they are. Dressing like
that…This Abraham in the Bible was going to kill his own kid for a
sacrifice. She gets nightmares from it, for God's sake! You call that
religion? Today a guy like that they'd lock him up. This is an age of
science, Eli. I size people's feet with an X-ray machine, for God's
sake. They've disproved all that stuff, Eli, and I refuse to sit by and
watch it happening on my own front lawn." The non-Jew who
expresses this view is essentially the prevalent view of the Jewish
American author, who has an uneasy relationship to the dogma of
Judaism, but feels some connection with common Jewish inherited
personality traits.

The existence of these traits are still present to this day, as we learn
from contemporary stories like Gary Schteyngart's "Lenny Hearts
Eunice," an excerpt from a five year old, dystopian novel about
the near future, where a recent Russian Jewish Immigrant, Lenny
Abramov, suffers from "interminable Jewishness." Like
Schteyngart, Lenny is a recent immigrant of Russia and kind of a
foil for his insecurities about assimilating into American life. In
this satire, Lenny's self-consciousness and intelligence (Jewish
stereotypes that he uses for comic effect) are enemies to him in
the future, where coolness and attractiveness are publicly gathered
and shared information quantified on tablets. Rather than
searching for immortality from religion, Lenny is of the belief he
can live forever with scientific advancement and works towards
this goal. In spite of his desire for eternal life, his sad reality is

mired by his own insecurity and narcissism. He comically remembers Jewish assimilation by describing his neighborhood. "I live in the last middle-class stronghold in the city, high atop a red-brick ziggurat that a Jewish garment workers' union erected on the banks of the East River back in the days when Jews sewed clothes for a living."

Lenny's world is entirely secular, but haunted by his Jewishness. The office he works was purchased by his boss, "Joshie (Weinberg)," and he "got it at auction for a mere eighty thousand dollars when the congregation folded after being bamboozled by some kind of Jewish pyramid scheme years ago." His office is a temple, a metaphor for the Jewish American ascension in business. Further he sees his insecurity about his Russian Jewishness everywhere he looks. It's an obstacle to his desire for eternal life ("All that Russian-Jewish testosterone is being turned right into dihydrotestosterone. That's killer stuff. Prostate cancer down the road."), and when his girlfriend kisses his Jewish nose, which of course he is insecure about, he sees himself as the elephant at the zoo. "Mother, aloneness, entrapment, extinction. The elephant is essentially an Ashkenazi animal." Though Lenny no longer has to deal with the systematic racism his ancestors felt, he is still burdened by his Jewishness.

Saul Bellow, from the previous generation, had to confront his anti-Semitism more directly than Schytengart, which may explain why he better masked his Jewish and Russian qualities. In the words of Christopher Hitchens, Saul Bellow, "In his own person he united the Jew, the cosmopolitan, the man of ideas, and the man of action." The son of Lithuanian Jewish parents, who had left a privileged life in St. Petersburg for Canada, he grew up in full observance of Jewish customs. In Bellow's own words, "At the age of four we began to read the Old Testament in Hebrew, we observed Jewish customs, some of them superstitions, and we recited prayers and blessings all day long. Because I had to memorize most of Genesis, my first consciousness was that of a cosmos, and in that cosmos I was a Jew." However, Bellow had a great desire, in spite of his heritage, noting in his autobiographical article "A Jewish Writer in America by Saul Bellow," that one of his goals was to disprove the myth that Jews were, "totally incapable of comprehending the Faustian spirit that had created the great civilization of the West." Bellow, who studied anthropology, mainly because he felt the English department at The University of Chicago was hugely anti-Semitic, was deeply concerned with spirituality and religion in his writing. However, he did not confine himself to Jewish thought.

"A Silver Dish" is a rich story that is about a son confronting his narcissistic con man of a father's death and the whole story of his hugely dysfunctional Jewish family that aside from his father had become fanatical Christians. More than that, it is a story about how the world has changed since, Woody's childhood in the depression and the uncertain reality of the 1970s. Directly after describing the actual physical repellence of Woody's father, Pop, the narrator creates a disturbed image of the world, "Think what times these are. The papers daily give it to you—the Lufthansa pilot in Aden is described by the hostages as being on his knees, begging the Palestinian terrorists not to execute him, but they shoot him through the head. Later they themselves are killed. And still others shoot others, or shoot themselves. That's what you read in the press, see on the tube, mention at dinner. We know now what goes daily through the whole of the human community, like a global death-peristalsis."

Interestingly, before telling a story that spans many decades about a Jewish family that was mostly converted into being born again

Christians, he speaks of a famous Palestinian plane hijacking, before comparing his father in his coffin to Ben Gurion, the first Israeli Prime Minister. Though his father was essentially an atheist, his Judaism is a part of him and his wish to buried amongst the Jews was granted. Even though he is clearly an amoral person, he holds onto the moral high ground, because he, unlike his ex-wife, doesn't make his children proselytize Evangelical Christianity. And though Woody had once been training to become a minister, he was an agnostic, deeply concerned with spiritual matters, much like Bellow himself.

Much like the perspectives offered in the story, the message is largely formless. What this family does clearly express is the hypocrisy of religious dogma. However dark and misguided the world seems to be, it is clearly reflected in the relationship between Woody and Pop, but in spite of it all, Bellow's story maintains hopefulness for a better world, even though it clearly notes that selfishness in this world is usually rewarded. "Pop was so selfish. It's usually the selfish people who are loved the most. They do what you deny yourself, and you love them for it. You give them your heart." Selfishness that is the direct inverse of what it means to be a Jew, who traditionally strove towards unity, love and selflessness.

Woody however does not love his father until he dies. Pop dies at the close of the story, but it is a cathartic death. Pop's willfulness is finally accepted by Woody and he is able to empathize with him, after years of discord that reached its peak when Pop stole a silver dish from a Scandinavian evangelical, leading to a violent fistfight. Maybe in that moment Woody realizes his true feeling about the universe that he noticed at the World's Fair as a child, "that the goal, the project, God's purpose was (and he couldn't explain why he thought so; all evidence was against it)—that this world should be a love world, that it should eventually recover and be entirely a world of love."

And really this is the ultimate goal of multiculturalism. Not to preach the dogma of one culture or another, but to show us how to have compassion for one another, by looking deeply at how unfair the world is for everyone and see what is preventing the world from becoming this "world of love." Jewish American authors were able to use their feeling of separation from American culture to express many deep truths about humanity. Authors like Bellow, Roth and Schteyngart attempt to look at the world nakedly to try and understand what it is to be human. The more specifically they dig into their own lives and the Jewishness steeped in their personalities, the more universal their work becomes.

IT SOUNDS ALRIGHT: T2 AND THE DEMISE OF CINEMA

Sick Boy: It's certainly a phenomenon in all walks of life.

Mark "Rent-boy" Renton: What do you mean?

Sick Boy: Well, at one time, you've got it, and then you lose it, and it's gone forever. All walks of life: George Best, for example. Had it, lost it. Or David Bowie, or Lou Reed…

Mark "Rent-boy" Renton: Some of his solo stuff's not bad.

Sick Boy: No, it's not bad, but it's not great either. And in your heart you kind of know that although it sounds all right, it's actually just shite.

Trainspotting 2 was arguably a better visual experience than Trainspotting. The acting was spot on, it was nostalgic, funny and emotionally effective. Still, Sick Boy's unifying theory of reality holds true. Trainspotting 2 was alright, but in the back of your mind you're thinking it's really shite.

Danny Boyle is a master of visuals and music. He knows how to stir emotion. He's not afraid of violence, sex and body fluids in a very sterile age in filmmaking. In spite of his advanced age (believe it or not the guy was 40 when T1 was released), his musical tastes are solid and much more contemporary than mine. He clearly has tremendous affection for the characters Irvine Welsh invented and he made iconic, which not only made Boyle and Ewan McGregor A-List iconoclasts for two decades, but encapsulated the Brit-pop era. Trainspotting defined the era.

Trainspotting felt like it was shot out of a cannon. Though I wasn't permitted to see the film in a theater, my mother, like many youngish expats living in Connecticut after years of boozing at Studio 54 and the Mud club had an itch to stay cool in spite of it all. As something of an Imperialism sympathetic romantic anglophile, our Range Rover blasted Iggy and Pulp in defiance of our Upper class suburban boredom. When HBO started playing Trainspotting in regular rotation, a new world opened before my eyes. Scotland, junk, Renton and especially Sick Boy began to inform my worldview. While most people remember the tragedy of the film it was lost on me. It was too cool and stylish. The music was too good for me to be caught up in the morality of the tale.

Though I wasn't popular, though it was all I desperately wanted, Trainspotting, my Kurt obsession and even my early devotion to Seinfeld coupled with a Gifted and Talented program IQ and poor grades confirmed that I was cooler than everyone else. Fast forward to my high school days living in New York, doing all matter of drugs developing even more esoteric tastes befriending beautiful young women who looked to me like a weird stoner brother, to college and obnoxiously pretentious alcoholism where I took pleasure in taking the piss out of people for the entertainment. I could not have been who I was without Danny Boyle, Irvine Welsh and Iggy Pop.

The problem with nostalgia is that it always feels stale. Nothing can ever be as meaningful as it was to you as a child. Even so, piss and blood aside, the culture is too sterile to make great films. While some people say "What about *Moonlight*," I would argue it's not even the best American film in a year of very bad films. *Manchester by the Sea* and *Nocturnal Animals* were way better.

Film is not entertainment, it's ideology. When all the viewers share the same ideology, we get beautifully made films like *Moonlight*, that are about gay sex without sexuality. When all the greats seemed to have lost their fastball the past few years (Scorcese (I'll give *Silence* another chance), The Coen Brothers), because in the back of your mind you're thinking this is shite, what hope is there for movies?

On Anti-Semitism

IN THE FACE OF TERROR WHAT CAN AMERICAN AND ISRAELI JEWS LEARN FROM ONE ANOTHER

The same things happen in Israel over and over. Yesterday at Sarona Market in Tel Aviv, an upscale shopping market was infiltrated when Muslim fundamentalists open-fired on innocent civilians. The attackers were dressed as ultra-Orthodox Jewish men in shiny suits to evade suspicion. Gunshots reigned over the market for about a minute. People gasped in a state of panic, running for cover, hiding under tables, as others found solace in a meat locker. Four were murdered and sixteen were wounded, including Asaf Bar, who miraculously survived two bullet wounds to the head. The brutality of this event was so unimaginably bleak and horrific; it hit a nerve with the international media, unlike the attacks that are happening throughout the country on average slightly more than every other day.

The terror here is constant and unrelenting. Even if you don't really feel it on a daily level it permeates through the air. There is always a sense something bad can happen behind the aesthetically challenged somewhat chic modern exterior and lively Tel Aviv lifestyle. Still, I was shocked looking at the recent terror figures.

In a time of relative peace since September 13th, 38 people have been killed in terrorist attacks and 466 people (including 4 Palestinians) injured. There have been 151 stabbing attacks (including 66 attempted attacks), 92 shootings, 43 vehicular (ramming) attacks and one vehicle (bus) bombing. This is perhaps why, less than 24 hours later, business is open with no remnants of the attack in plain sight. While Israelis are horrified and saddened by the news, they live on and continue. They won't allow the terrorists to win. They refuse to live in fear. This is nothing new for them. Almost everyone has experienced this sort of tragedy falling upon someone they love, a family member, or someone they went to school with in their lifetime, whether it is from someone dying in the army or being killed randomly in terror. This is precisely why Israel is offended when an American, even an American Jew has any critical stance on Israel. "They don't live here, so they don't know."

As an American living in Israel, this tragic event and a wonderful Jonathan Safran Foer story entitled "Maybe it was the Distance," made me consider the inherent differences between Israel and America, specifically what divides Israeli and American Jews. I still find it baffling that a Jewish man within a hair's breadth of the Democratic nomination who worked on an Israeli kibbutz made pronouncements that Israel was disproportionate in its defense in the war with Gaza last year and it got me thinking about why the world hates Israel so much.

The extreme left in America works under the assumption that Israel is doing something wrong in Gaza, while the common-sense answer is that Israel is defending itself from a terrorist Hamas government. However, in the politically correct landscape of the world today, Israel is viewed as an Imperialist nation and exclusively to blame for the plight of Palestinians. In this picture,

Hamas is not to blame for using its billions of dollars of aid from around the world, including from Israel itself to build tunnels to attack Israel, while firing rockets from highly populated areas. Jordan and all the other Arab countries who don't offer Palestinian refugees aid should not be blamed for taking the land that was mandated by Great Britain as the landmass Palestine (though they took a lot more of the "Imperialist" Israel). Of course, there is also the false belief that Jews didn't live in the territory Palestine before Israel's Independence was proclaimed in 1948.

While I'm aware it is silly to make pronouncements of fact on the issue that impedes upon the narrative that Israel is evil, because no one will listen, I strive to understand how the narrative of Israeli oppression on the level of apartheid has gained steam with American liberals and Jews. Maybe by understanding the cause of this misunderstanding, the means of fixing this problem of public relations will reveal itself. I have a hard time remembering what I thought Israel was like before I visited Israel, but I'm not sure I had any idea what I was walking into. I knew Haifa was supposed to be the Silicon Valley of the Middle East and Tel Aviv was the Paris, but neither of these assumptions do the cities justice, and in spite of hearing such sentiments, I was half-expecting to see something more Middle Eastern, with dirt roads and camels.

I hadn't the slightest idea what Israel and Israelis were like other than the stereotypes of haggling electronics storeowners I had grown up amongst as a child of New York City and what I had read in literature. The women were supposed to be tough and beautiful. In *Portnoy's Complaint,* I read about the title character Alexander Portnoy's ass being kicked by a beautiful soldier kibbutznik after she refused his advances and her shaming of him for being self-deprecating, essentially the main feature of Jewish

American humor. In her kibbutz lifestyle, Israeli unity was a large ingredient. Arguing with a self-deprecating and sexually ashamed American Jews she describes what it is to live in a kibbutz, where she says, "inherently the system in which I participate (and voluntarily, that is crucial too—voluntarily!), that that system is humane and just. As long as the community owns the means of production, as long as all needs are provided by the community, as long as no man has the opportunity to accumulate wealth or to live off the surplus value of another man's labor, then the essential character of the kibbutz is being maintained. No man is without dignity. In the broadest sense, there is equality. And that is what matters most."

While very few could argue that this sentiment is the predominant one in Israeli culture today, it still permeates. Israelis still feel united to one another and dependent on each other, even though they have a difficult time trusting the cashier will give them correct change. If someone passes out, gets hit by a car, or even just needs directions, a crowd of people trying to help the person, while in New York, the impulse is to ignore others and only help if it seems absolutely necessary.

Many Israelis see American Jews as spoiled, self-centered, materialistic, and are skeptical of their Judaism (reform Judaism is not acknowledged as Judaism, if your mother was not Jewish you're not Jewish, what the heck is a female rabbi?). Many don't understand self-deprecating Jewish humor, nor do they wish to, as American Jews have no interest in how much of a struggle it is for a middle class Israeli family to survive. American Jews, who are liberal, are still guided by self-interest a lot more than the kibbutzim of the 1960s.

On the other side of the coin, many Israelis are brutally

materialistic, would live in America in a second if they could and latch onto American culture like a mosquito to a lightbulb. Israeli Jews are endowed with a hardness and seriousness absent in American Jews. They take themselves extremely seriously and don't show their weakness freely. They are also extremely suspicious of one another. Israeli society like American society is racked with contradictions, though the self-assurance of the Israeli character is more black and white, less self-analytical, which is why the Israeli tech millionaire in Safran Foer's story can say with a straight face that "The best Italian food in the world is in Israel." When his American cousin calls BS on his pronouncement, he says that the best Italian food doesn't have to be from Italy, because bagels are a Jewish food and the best bagels are in New York City. When terror comes into play, the pronouncements are even bolder and more personal. "You don't know, because you don't live here" is a general calling card and though they are 90% percent correct about Israeli policy, many young American Jews focuses on the 10% where Israel is wrong and can't get past the cultural differences.

This mixture of Israeli assuredness and Hamas' strategy of firing from populated areas and not evacuating buildings Israel announces they are destroying in warfare paints a picture of Israel as the oppressor. Not understanding the politically correct climate of the world the Israeli government has made tone-deaf public service cartoons mocking Palestine's tunnels and their shame killing of homosexuals. With arrogant gaffes like this—that expressly illustrate the Israeli lack of understanding of progressive American culture and Hamas' ingenious though despicable strategy of putting its civilians in harm's way—Israel looks like they seek the genocide of Gaza and that they have no respect for other cultures.

It also doesn't help that those who most openly advocate on Israel's behalf, people like Ted Cruz and Sarah Palin, are the most opposite to the largely secular liberal American Jew. American liberal Jews can't help but feel, "If they disagree on everything else, they must be wrong about Israel too." American Jews with their nuanced political opinions are immediately turned off by Israeli self-assuredness and it is a matter of taste more than anything else.

These confusions of culture are really huge impediments to improving the relationship between Israel and America. If American Jews and Israelis cannot budge and learn to care for another, warts and all, above their differences in culture and opinion, the survival of Judaism and Israel will be in danger. It is the responsibility of the Jewish people to repair the world and this begins with a choice to unite with one another. While the majority of Jews in Israel and America believe they have some shared destiny, this will only be felt in a meaningful way if we make efforts to understand one another. Connection between these two distinctly individualistic people who look the same and have more in common than they think will be the root of our salvation. These horrific tragedies that befall on Israel, like it or not are tied to American Jews as well. Jews are always blamed for the crises that plague the world and if we are not connected to one another we will never transcend that hatred. When something particularly tragic, like the events of yesterday happen, I request American Jews like myself to stand strong with Israel publicly to make a communal action of love together, which will combat the media's portrayal of Israel as an Imperialist apartheid state.

REPAIRING A BROKEN WORLD

The world is broken and wants to be whole again. Maybe this is the source of the prominence of the Talmudic phrase Tikkun Olam, meaning literally, "to repair the world," that has lately been popularized by many prominent Jewish people and organizations. While I find it admirable that many Jews latch onto tikkun olam, for charitable pursuits and innovations in noble fields like medical research, the world is demanding something greater from His chosen people. According to the wisdom of Kabbalah, it is the role of the Jewish people to repair the world, by teaching the world to connect properly, offering an example to illustrate the oneness of all of creation to gradually lift the world to a state of sanctity.

Baal HaSulam, the most influential Kabbalist of the 20th century once wrote, "In my opinion, there is only one soul in the world." Thus, the error Jews make is only a function of our perception wherein, "one feels one's soul as a unique organ." Sadly, this problem of perception creates a splintered faith of incongruous values, driven by individual egos. It is all but forgotten that unity was once viewed as a necessity to devote one's self to God. Jews throughout our history wanted to mirror the foundation of Israel roughly 3400 years ago, where a people who stood behind Moses "as one man and one heart" to receive the Torah. Even as other nations sought the destruction of Israel and its descendants, they held firm to these values.

Today, in places like my country of America where Jews have relative security and prosperity, the unity disintegrates. While history confirms this peace will not hold forever, it would be wise to find commonality before grave danger comes. People always find it easier to unite around the negative, but why not focus on the solution? It would be best to focus on connection in times of relative peace, where the hatred against Jews does not present imminent danger. Unfortunately, this creates a difficult dichotomy.

The Creator, in his infinite wisdom, clearly has sense of humor. On the surface, there is no group less likely than contemporary Jews to unite under a single ideal without severe external pressure. It's difficult to miss that Jewish people tend to argue over every nuance of everything. Hence the expression, "put two Jews in a room and you'll get three opinions." In spite of this inherent trait, just a few decades ago there once was a notable exception. The state of Israel seemed to symbolize great meaning and ideals that were nearly universally respected. Ben Gurion, Golda Meir and Moshe Dayan, were Israeli political celebrities and symbols of ideals trying to bring the world something new and essential. It greatly saddens me that in today's political landscape, the one thing American Jews universally cared for and agreed upon has become a bitter source of division.

While liberal Jews often cite Bibi Netanyahu and his policies as the source of their problems with the Jewish state, there is a much more sinister trend developing. American Jews, especially those of the younger generation, have slowly lost their Jewish identity and have thus become indifferent to Israel, once again indicating that without strong opposition, unity is a difficult proposition. They no longer see a state aspiring to idealism out of the shadows of the Holocaust, but an oppressive regime who as Bernie Sanders notes ad-nauseum uses "disproportionate force," when forced to defend itself. Rather than contest the rampant rise of anti-Semitism and pleas for boycotts of Israel on college campuses, many young Jews find themselves sympathizing with the plight of Hamas led Palestinians. If they do support Israel, many young reform and secular Jews find themselves backstepping in their appraisal of the state, taking pride in their individual, highly nuanced perspectives that conform to liberal American values over Jewish values, at the liberal universities Jews like me find themselves attending, where atheism is an unofficial rule of thumb.

In concert with the gradual loss of Jewish values, Americans have also lost their desire for unity. There's no clear profit in it. Today, Jews in America and throughout the world see themselves as individuals and have thrived in their pursuits over the last century or so. Look no further than the statistic that 22 percent of the world's Nobel Prizes have been awarded to Jews, though they make up .2 percent of the world's population. To put that in perspective, a Jew is 110 times more likely to win a Nobel Prize than a non-Jew. Not to mention 55 times more likely to be worth over a billion dollars.

With this success, some Jewish people feel they have been endowed with a special opportunity to repair the world through charitable acts and virtuous accomplishments, but in reality, this isn't bringing the connection the world desperately needs. In spite of the achievements of the Jewish people and their desire to improve the world, tikkun olam (repairing the world) has not even begun to take shape in any discernible way. Disproportionate wealth is decimating the American dream, the environment is on the brink of a full-scale collapse, racism and anti-Semitism (often disguised as anti-Zionism) is a perpetual threat. War, famine, disease and genocide thrive across the globe. In America, every other person is either drunk or stoned or on anti-depressants. Many people feel a constant sense of unease, burdened by irrational fears and endless sufferings.

What Jews need to understand is that this suffering is purposeful. Humanity is at odds with the natural world, where everything works for the benefit of the whole. The system of nature is crying out for us to overcome our egos. People conversely are driven by the desire to receive pleasure, and thus work only for the benefit of themselves and subconsciously dominate others to feed their egos. The only way to combat this selfish nature and feel whole is to connect to others, but precisely because of the egoistic nature of man, humanity resists this connection with more separation at all costs.

While many Jewish people of all ages will have hotly contested debates over the state of Israel at Passover Seders, the goal should be to remember the real meaning of Israel.

Israel is not a place, but an ideal. It is a desire to connect above the forces of separation. In today's world where a person can literally turn off opposing points of view on his or her Facebook page, the bravest thing one can do is listen to another person with his or her heart without the blinders of his or her ego. By awakening the heart above the mind in an effort to reunite into a single soul, a person is taking a giant leap towards repairing the world, for this is the first step in true connection. If the Jewish people around the world could connect around the ideal of Israel, rather than bicker over the democracy lodged in the Middle East, it could create a ripple effect that has the power to transform humanity. When people choose to serve a great cause in connection above their small egotistical desire, they have the capacity to be great themselves and shape a better world.

HATRED OF ISRAEL IS JEW HATRED: IT HAS NOTHING TO DO WITH THE JERUSALEM EMBASSY

America is under attack from both internal and external forces guided by Islamic extremism. Monday, a 27-year-old Bangladeshi immigrant, Akayed Ullah, detonated an unsuccessful suicide bomb in my hometown subway system. This is the second terror attack in Manhattan in the last six weeks. On Halloween, eight were murdered in a Grand Theft Auto style killing rampage by Sayfullo Saipov who murdered eight cyclists by running them over on a bike path with a flatbed truck. Though the extent of the collusion with the organization is a bit fuzzy, both incidents were connected to ISIS, if only to the extent that both of the legal immigrants attested to their allegiance to the terrorist organization. Saipov was radicalized in the borders of the United States, while my former neighbor, Kensington Brooklyn resident, Akayed Ullah, appears based solely on the sniff test and neighbor's testimony, to have always been of an extreme religious bent. This week's pathetic and pathetically executed attack by Ullah was particularly emblematic of the times, as he cited recent bombings and tensions in Gaza as the reason for the attack, after Trump's announcement of his recognition of the capital of Israel as the capital of Israel to distract us from truly abhorrent anti-Semitism.

One example of explicit Jew hatred occurred last Friday in Times Square. A large protest, ostensibly about Trump's Jerusalem announcement, became a chant for violence and the destruction of the state of Israel. It's not unusual for pro-Palestinian supporters to chant for the destruction of the state of Israel with lines like "We don't want no two state – we want 48," and "From the river to the Sea, Palestine will be free." Just as it's not all that unusual for these protestors to call for terror attacks with lines like their rallying cry, "There is only one solution – Intifada revolution," suggesting something not unlike Hitler's final solution.

While these above protest calls are truly horrific, unusually this protest became even more sinister as the Muslim protestors shouted, "Jews, remember Khaybar – the army of Muhammad is returning." What the protestors were referring to was Mohammed's 7th century massacre of Jews and they are explicitly calling for Jews to be massacred. As The Board of Deputies of British Jews elucidated after the London version of the protest the same day, "The 'Khybar, Khybar' chant heard and documented at Friday's protest outside the US Embassy in London can only be interpreted as a call to incite violence against Jewish people. It is outrageous that these protesters thought that such a chant would be acceptable on the streets of London in 2017. That this comes in the context of a firebombing of a synagogue in Sweden and an attack on a kosher restaurant in Amsterdam only increases our concern. These acts are not criticisms of a decision by the US government but demonstrations of anti-Semitism." If anyone thought the Palestinian state was a territorial political war and not a religious war aimed at killing Jews, this protest and similar protests across Europe show us the true intention of anti-Zionism.

Though it should be clear to all, that the root of anti-Zionism is anti-Semitism deeply steeped in Islamic fanaticism, cut to

Newsweek's front page where Trump is blamed for a steep rise in anti-Semitism, particularly in Europe.

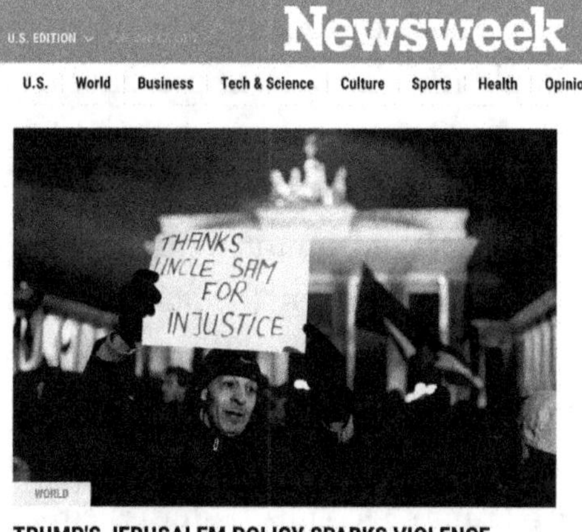

TRUMP'S JERUSALEM POLICY SPARKS VIOLENCE AGAINST JEWS

The article on the previous page had another ludicrous title, "BECAUSE OF TRUMP, PEOPLE ARE BURNING ISRAELI FLAGS AND ATTACKING JEWS." Though Trump is not to blame, in Germany 12 were arrested as they burned flags, and in Malmö, 200 Palestinians were shouting, "Shoot the Jews," just after masked men firebombed a temple in another Swedish city, Gothenburg.

How a major mainstream magazine like Newsweek, would blame Trump for Islamic extremists shouting "Shoot the Jews," is a mystery me. As I wrote last week, it certainly has nothing to do with Jerusalem as the Palestinian Liberation Army explicitly called for the destruction of Israel, in the 60s, when Jordanian Palestinians controlled Jerusalem and Jews were forbidden to enter most of Jerusalem, including the Wailing Wall. The Palestinians will not rest until all of Israel is theirs, preferably killing as many Jews as possible in the process and they're not even hiding it anymore.

The Jerusalem decision is only an excuse for the anti-Semitism that has existed for thousands of years. Jerusalem has been the capital and spiritual center of Judaism for 3,000 years and has always been hotly debated and a source of friction. This week as Jews celebrate Chanukah, we should recognize the importance of the city that the Maccabees fought the Greeks to protect. While Jews in America may be divided about nuances of Israeli policy, the understandably confusing election of Donald Trump and a bevy of other topics, as Jews it is our responsibility to unite behind Israel, the one place Jews were given sanctuary after the Holocaust and during the expulsion of nearly a million Jews from Arab countries. Terrorists and those chanting to kill us cannot dictate our policies. No matter what you think of Trump, recognizing Jerusalem as the eternal capital of the Jewish people should be a non-partisan issue.

WHY ANTI-SEMITES THRIVE IN ACADEMIA

Hatem Bazian, Source: Wikipedia commons

The Berkeley Professor and Palestinian activist, Hatem Bazian, has been embroiled in controversy since retweeting posts equating Israel to North Korea and Nazis. While he has apologized for the tweets as a careless mistake, Jewish students and fifteen professors have petitioned for his dismissal. It is one of many blatant anti-Semitic incidents in his history. Though a relative unknown, even academic circles, under the radar Bazian has been crucial to the dissemination of anti-Zionist thought for over two decades, first as a graduate student and now as a professor.

The sad reality is that little is likely to happen. Two weeks have passed since the campaign began and it looks like the story has already slipped through the cracks. Bazian will probably continue at Berkeley, reputation untarnished.

The retweet of a meme portraying an Orthodox Jew cast against the words "Mom, LOOK! I IS CHOSEN! I CAN NOW KILL, RAPE, SMUGGLE ORGANS & STEAL THE LAND OF PALESTINIANS YAY #ASHKE-NAZI" is appalling. However, Bazian's explicit and implicit history of Jew hatred is even more worrying. It expresses the total acceptance of anti-Semitism by academia and the means by which anti-Zionism disguised as anti-Semitism is sold to trusting students through lies and innuendo.

As a graduate student in 1992, Bazian accused SFSU's paper the *Golden Gater* of being a haven for Jewish spies and encouraged fellow protestors to "Take a look at the type of names on the buildings around campus (UC Berkeley)— Haas, Zellerbach — and decide who controls this university (in 2002)." Sermonizing in 1999, he suggested that massacring Jews was a necessity for his faith, by quoting, "In the Hadith, the Day of Judgment will never happen until you fight the Jews. They are on the west side of the river, which is the Jordan River, and you're on the east side until the trees and stones will say, 'oh Muslim, there is a Jew hiding behind me. Come and kill him!'."

Aside from spreading Jewish conspiracy theories and Jew hatred masked as theology, Bazian is a champion of the BDS movement, falsely claiming that Israel is a colonial apartheid state (Israel is a refugee state), while he directly campaigns for intifada against Israel in the Middle East and the United States. While intifada is a vague term meaning something to the effect of uprising, the first two intifadas account for the death of over a thousand innocent Israeli citizens and over ten-thousand injuries.

Let's take a look at a few absurd statements Bazian has made throughout the years with responses in bold. The first two are alternative histories that don't contain even a kernel of truth and the third is a call for terrorism:

"Israel provoked the Six-Day War in 1967, and it was not fighting for survival"

— Hatem Bazian, **Twitter**, June 3, 2017

Egypt blocked the Straits of Tiran, international water and Israel's main trade route, where Israel imported 90% of their oil, while under attack by Palestinian guerilla armies in Syria and Jordan. Israel was clearly fighting for its survival.

"Historical evidence does not support Zionist claims re the Western Wall."

— Hatem Bazian, **Twitter**, December 20, 2016

King Herod built the Western Wall in 20BCE, to expand the Second Temple. If you need archaeological evidence, see the

"DKA LYH seal – In 2011, Archaeologist Eli Shukrun found a tiny fired clay object stamped with an inscription consisting of the Hebrew letters ליה דכא… Talmudic scholar, Prof. Shlomo Naeh, convincingly showed that this is a unique object that was used as a token/voucher that enabled the Temple administrator priests to keep track of commerce related to sacrificial offerings. This practice is documented in the Mishna, the first written redaction of Jewish Oral Law dating to around 200 CE (Shekalim 5: 3-5)." (source:https://templemount.wordpress.com/2016/10/14/archaeological-proof-of-the-jewish-temples-on-the-temple-mount/)

"How come we don't have an intifada in this country (The United States)? … and it's about time that we have an intifada in this country that change[s] fundamentally the political dynamics in here. And we know…they're gonna say it's some Palestinian being too radical, well you haven't seen radicalism yet!"

— Hatem Bazian, San Francisco Rally, 2004

We don't have an intifada in the United States, because it's an act of terrorism if not outright war directed at a minority group.

The above beliefs and history makes one beg the question, how is a blatantly hateful anti-Semite a professor at one of America's most prestigious public Universities? Also of concern is how a professor at a publicly funded University is able to present alternate fake history as fact. The reason is the direct result of professors like Bazian propagating the idea that Israel is a colonial power.

Speaking to like-minded people, he outlines the strategy clearly by preaching, "We need to make a link between what is taking place today in Palestine and the whole transnational, anti-colonial, anti-slavery, and anti-oppression struggle." He is a propagandist posing as an advocate for oppressed people, who feels the ends always justify the means.

Bazian gets away with spreading lies by selling the narrative Muslims are a greatly oppressed people whose acts of terrorism are divorced from religious doctrine. The means by which he is able to legitimize people spreading horrific anti-Semitic doctrine is by labeling all critique of his religion as racism with the word Islamophobia. Islamophobia is a subject he just so happens to teach courses on. Thus, there is a climate where we see people in the media like Somalian Muslim Refugee turned Dutch MP, Ayaan Hirsi Ali, speaking out against the horrors of Islam labeled as bigots. If someone criticizes any aspect of Islam they are not only "culturally insensitive," they are "Islamophobic," a word that is now interchangeable with racist. If you are accused of being a racist in America your life is often destroyed.

Anti-Semitism has always existed. It flares up at certain times throughout history. Lately, cloaked as anti-Zionism, anti-Semitism has caught like a forest fire in California. Israel and the Jewish people can no longer kowtow to those who want them dead. When people with power, like Bazian, and as I wrote last week, many others are using dirty tactics to claim Israel has no right to exist, the stakes are too high. Jews around the world need to unite in their shared history and defend Israel in spite of the differences in opinions that divide them. When the Jewish people and their supporters are united against a common foe, the Jewish people can redeem themselves and strengthen. However, when Jews stand back idly and fight against their own interests they seem to always strengthen their enemies and compromise their own ability to survive and thrive.

THE HOLOCAUST AND THE WORLD TO COME

"I go back inside the train; I carry out dead infants; I unload luggage. I touch corpses, but I cannot overcome the mounting, uncontrollable terror. I try to escape from the corpses, but they are everywhere: lined up on the gravel, on the cement edge of the ramp, inside the cattle cars. Babies, hideous naked women, men twisted by convulsions. I run off as far as I can go, but immediately a whip slashes across my back. Out of the corner of my eye I see an S.S. man, swearing profusely. I stagger forward and run, lose myself in the Canada group. Now, at last, I can once more rest against the stack of rails. The sun has leaned low over the horizon and illuminates the ramp with a reddish glow; the shadows of the trees have become elongated, ghostlike. In the silence that settles over nature at this time of day, the human cries seem to rise all the way to the sky."

Tadeusz Borowski, This Way for the Gas, Ladies and Gentleman

"What happened to the Germans is one of nature's wonders. They were considered among the most civilized nations, and all of a sudden, overnight, they became savages, the worst among the most primitive nations in history. Moreover, Hitler was elected by the majority's vote."

Baal Hasulam - The Solution

The Holocaust was maybe the greatest tragedy in the history of the world. When people see something so abhorrent, they can't help but wonder how it was allowed to happen. There are both historical and psychological explanations that begin to scratch the surface of how such tragedy was possible, but no definitive answer. There is no clear answer as to why this became tolerable, but as Kabbalists know, it is the result of the general rise of the ego across the world. Germany had developed itself as far as it could on a corporeal level, before an Upper Force destroyed the nation and the only people left to blame were us, the Jews.

With the wisdom of Kabbalah, the world is simplified. Everything is about the push and pull of the ego. With this knowledge, we see The Holocaust not as a result of socioeconomic consequences and the will of Adolph Hitler, but as an inevitable event in the history of mankind. When Hitler took power in 1933, he alluded to the Jews and how they must be abdicated, logically uttering, "A nation must have no discord." He saw man's natural inclination towards hating Jews and exploited this inherent vice in all men. Something about Jews made them distrustful easy targets, and while many people were not actively anti-Semitic, the lunacy of Hitler's claims about Jews had very little opposition. They quickly gained steam. If Jews were beloved this would not have been possible. It is easy to confuse this tragedy as the result of Hitler's charisma and will, but we must remember even Hitler's foes would not help us in 1938 when Hitler offered us to all the countries that participated in The League of Nations. Slowly, Hitler's anti-Semitic allusions perverted scientific reasoning to build a theory about our people to prove we were not human.

While "The Final Solution," was not immediately advertised as a mission to extinguish the Jews, most of their Aryans slowly fell in line, beneath the veneer of ideology. The work camps were being built for The Jews to occupy and the Germans along with the Jews were blindsided when Jews all across Europe were forced to leave their homes to occupy them. These slave camps were built like legitimate factories to support the German war effort. While there may have been utterances that these factories were part of the solution to The Jewish Problem, it was not something openly spoken of. Jews were almost universally despised at this point, but like the camps themselves the thought of the atrocities were set aside from the landscape of German life.

By 1939, all Jews in Germany were wearing Jewish stars and were to be enslaved for the war effort. Every single possession of these two million people was stolen and itemized, before leaving their middle-class homes for the cesspool known as the ghettoes. The only reminder of these people were the millions of suitcases the Nazi army seized containing everything of value the Jews owned. There were fur coats, jewelry, gold watches, paintings, cufflinks made of teeth, furniture, books. All the signs of a sophisticated and powerful people. The Germans organized these valuable possessions and recorded their findings. The items were seized, recorded, used and sold.

Everything about the Nazis was systematic and precise. Maybe it made killing their neighbors easier. Following detailed and specific orders could distract Nazis from the evil they were exercising. There was no time to look at the bigger picture. All that time devoted to following and executing orders left little time to process what they were doing. The stain of Judaism was disappearing one diamond ring at a time.

The six million deaths that took place over three years is an imperceptible event. All of Europe was stained with the blood of our ancestors. In the words of Joseph Stalin, "A single death is a tragedy, a million deaths is a statistic." The Holocaust was six million tragedies, a figure that overwhelms. As human beings, we cannot comprehend the horror of this. We don't know what six million people looks like, but when we see the indignities of a single camp—the bodies dropped haphazardly like rocks in a pile, we feel overwhelming disgust. The horror lives within all of us, but it is denied in our conscious comprehension of the world. We do not see the women and children being executed and separated from each other on a daily basis, because it would be too painful. Instead, the terror lives in our subconscious. The spirit of bloodshed is covered by the artifice of societies, hiding the spiritual world from our perception with our egos and wrong desires.

What seems obvious logically, but no one chooses to infer from this event is that then entire world was tacitly agreeing with Hitler's view of the Jews. We choose not to believe it, just as we choose not to face the horrors of The Holocaust on a daily basis. We deny that if there had been a single state willing to take on our highly educated, uncommonly successful population, The Holocaust would never have happened. If Jews were not despised it would be common sense for a suffering nation to take in a wealthy segment of the German population in times of grave economic turmoil.

We were viewed as manipulative and less than human not just by Hitler, but the entire world. We were a defective race of selfish self-seekers who raped the lands we inhabited for ourselves and horded our wisdom for ourselves. There was no reason for us to exist in their disturbed worldview. And though it is hidden behind a veneer, people still feel this today. They see that the Jews do not fulfill their role in the correction of the world.

Further, and perhaps even more alarming was that Hitler was completely inessential to The Holocaust. It was an inevitable cataclysm in Jewish history. Germany was inessential. It was the result of the way the world viewed Jews. They are inherently distrustful of Jews, because we were once united and do not share the method of unity that will cure the suffering of the world.

If it had not happened in Germany it would have happened elsewhere, and it can happen again. In the world before globalization, our egos manifested themselves in nationalism. After our egos could no longer handle being subjugated to Kings, our inflated egos attached themselves to self-determined nations. No nation was able to accept Judaism, because we were viewed as a different species, somehow special and separate. Let us not forget that we are different. We are capable of shifting the landscape of the entire world. In the words of Leo Tolstoy, "The Jew is the symbol of eternity. ...He is the one who for so long had guarded the prophetic message and transmitted it to all mankind. A people such as this can never disappear. The Jew is eternal. He is the embodiment of eternity."

If the Jews were to unite above their differences, rather than just spread their Torah, they could end this cycle of suffering. In each and every generation we are tested. Let us hope in our lifetime we can unite the nation of Israel and lead the rest of the world by example. We will see religion as we know it today is inessential. All we will want is a stronger connection.

We are the chosen people given the one essential truth to create a harmonious world, who for centuries have acknowledged our own suffering. Why do we allow it to continue as anti-Semitism blazes across the globe? Today the world is crying out for everyone to connect, regardless of their religion. Not all the Jews are required to unite as one, but we do need a force of light built by those who want to achieve eternity in this lifetime, be a part of "the world to come."

Though Jews once held this position of balancing the world in the spiritual realms, anyone who with a desire can connect to the original ideology of Judaism. Judaism has nothing to do with nationality, as the tribes that followed Abraham were culturally and racially diverse people clung to a message of hope and a single Creator. A message of unity that was again bestowed to The Hebrews after escaping Egyptian enslavement. The Israelites were a desire to be united for the sake of correcting the world. They achieved this state of selflessness, by building a force of light through binding together as one in concert with the Creator. This force, once again will cover all the hate in the world with love.

Kabbalah Articles

OPPOSITE FORCES

The Creator is pulling us towards him whether we know it or not. The natural development of the world is in opposition to the Creator, but this opposition is the necessary obstacle to knowing Him. While the Creator like nature, is the force of goodness and infinite giving known as bestowal, humanity is pulled by the force of the ego. The ego is constantly seeking pleasure for itself, often in seemingly contradictory forms. Out of this desire to enjoy, one ultimately destroys one's self and everything he or she connects with or comes across.

Kabbalah teaches one how to invert this desire for pleasure into a desire to bestow, a desire to be selfless, above one's default nature in equivalence with the desire of the Creator. This desire lifts a person above this world.

The difficulty inborn in lifting one's self above this world is its contrast to everything that one can sense in reality. To rise into spirituality one has to be foolish and stubborn. He or she has to live in an environment that champions one working above his or her natural desire.

Additionally, one has to be aided by the Creator, so he or she will not lose their connection to this environment. This person who the Creator shows favor to has to work honestly, do everything in one's power to forego the limitations of his or her rational mind, by purporting to care about more about others than themselves, until it becomes a reality. Then they need to lose this love as the Creator shows them self-love in the same measure. They need to understand that this desire to love others is a lie and an impossibility.

They must learn that only the Creator can forge a path to make the impossible possible. Only the Creator can turn hate into love to make one love others more than they love themselves. This work to do something unreasonable is the process of building the Creator, the remedy for a world where humanity's nature is leading us on a path to destroy ourselves.

2000 years ago, when Rabbi Shimon and his students wrote the Zohar, they achieved spiritual perfection, the complete attainment of the five spiritual worlds. They harnessed that light in their writings, so that when things got so bad there were no other options, when the collective ego of humanity would become so large that humanity would reach a state of hopelessness, that the remedy would exist for egoists to hasten the salvation of a broken world. Through the writings of the Ari and the interpretations by Baal HaSulam and his son the Rabash, humanity was given a clear pathway to this noble goal. We can build the light of the Creator under the instructions of a great Rav (Rabbi) by seeing the Creator in our connection with each other above our reason, sacrificing our desires to live in infinite pleasure. As I see it, the time is now.

THE END OF SUFFERING: HOW CONNECTION CURES EVERYTHING

I have dedicated my life to the study of the universal laws that operate the world. More specifically, my days have been spent exploring the relationship between the laws of nature and human existence. In my study, I have found the solution to the apparent dichotomy between nature and human relationships. Like the rest of the world, if I had not been taught how the system of the world operates, it would baffle me to look at the state of people today. In spite of the perfect order and beauty of the natural world, human beings continue to suffer.

What became clear to me in my years of study is that if humanity were able to learn a lesson from nature we would be able to bridge the gap between our imperfect lives and the natural world where everything depends upon everything else. We would naturally possess the remedy for all of our troubles. The world would see plainly that the key to solving every problem that comes our way is human connection and mutual dependence. Once we could truly live our lives for the benefit of others, we would as a byproduct love each other and create a sustainable future.

I can attest this isn't as easy as it sounds. My book, *The Egotist*, goes into great length examining the obstacles of absorbing connection as a medicine for suffering. As a former addict, I resisted connection, even in my recovery, until I was absorbed into a society that works painstakingly in the direction of better human relationships. Nevertheless, given the scope of my claim, you may be taken aback by the simplicity of my solution.

Human connection isn't exactly a revolutionary idea. In our globalized world, many people are aware we live in an interdependent system and connection is a word permeating through the air. Further, very few people would argue that connection is bad for society and we are beginning to sense that we need each other to restore our world to a better state.

If this is the case, what prevents us from realizing this connection? Why do our problems appear to us as unsalvageable? In spite of a desire to lead happy, fulfilling lives, we fight unnecessary wars and hate one another on the basis of nationalities, races and religions. Addiction spreads like wildfire. Families are destroyed by divorce at record rates and depression thrives like a virus. In the process of personal suffering, we do our best to destroy the ecosystem, the very planet that feeds and nourishes us. On the other side of the coin, when we look at nature, we see a vast, endlessly complex system that operates upon perfect rules where everything is dependent on everything else. What prevents humanity from achieving our own state of perfection? Why do we insist on destroying ourselves?

The reason we are not able to lead mutually fulfilling lives is because we fail to recognize the greatness of the self-sustaining system we live in and the oppositeness of man to the system. We don't recognize that if we were able to adapt to the flow of the world, we would live a life of endless fulfilment, because we would be tapped into the universe's endless abundance. While nature is perpetually achieving a balance between the two forces of connection and separation, because of the ego, individuals only work for their own benefit in separation.

As is plainly written in Genesis, "And the Lord saw that the wickedness of man was great in the earth, and that all the impulse of the thoughts of his heart was only evil continually. And the

Lord repented that He had made man on the earth, and it grieved Him at His heart."

This isn't exactly new knowledge, but as the world becomes more complex, we fool ourselves into believing the cancer of our own egos. Because of our innate wickedness, on our own we will never be able to overcome our selfish and assuredly destructive nature as much as we'd like to help others. Like we learned from Eve, the serpent will continue to live within us and reveal himself at the worst times. We will not be able to approach a new level of reality necessary for us to share all the abundance in the world together.

I have discovered a very useful tool to combat the serpent inside us. This tool allows us to tap into our collective wisdom and intuition, bypassing our negative nature. This method consists of discussion circles where people from diverse backgrounds discuss complicated issues to come to mutual solutions that are possible through connection in a roundtable workshop.

The rules of the workshop are very simple. One person asks a question about a practical problem that plagues them and the others in the circle do their best to answer the question and listen to the answers of the other people with their whole heart, as opposed to their minds. It is important for the people in the circle to never criticize the other person, or reject what the person has to say. There are no interruptions. All one must do is listen.

By making this small annulment of the ego, the circle almost always comes to a new understanding. A new force that was just an hour earlier hidden from reality comes to the surface. It becomes clear that out of this connection and a desire towards mutual dependence, we have the power to transform ourselves to understand and love each other. We become the owners of this force that has the power to transform the nature of man.

In a corrected world, we would recognize the importance of this structure and what we could learn from the wisdom of the circle. It would be self-evident that the cloud of our ego is preventing our fulfilment, blinding us from the wisdom of our hearts. It would be clear to all that the very structure of the world is a corrupted system that requires new ways of thinking and strategies to return to compassion. And while things may improve from time to time, none of these improvements will have any meaning as long as we are enslaved to our wiring that tells us to destroy others for our own benefit.

AN ALTERNATIVE TO PLEASURE SEEKING

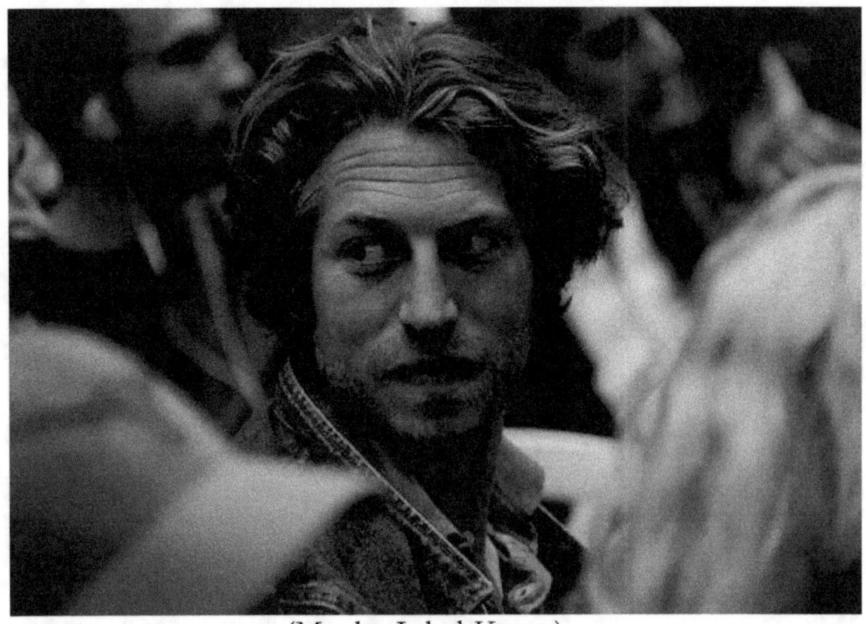

(Me, by Inbal Kaner)

We all seek to profit from one another. It is the very nature of the capitalist system we live in. On an interpersonal level, we seek the comfort of others, because in the best moments they make us feel good. While this, in and of itself, is OK, we see that in spite of our best intentions, our desire to feel good and to make those close to us feel good, does not profit society or ourselves. While some people are for the most part happy, for the majority and even for the seemingly very happy people amongst us, to live is to suffer. What if the reason for our suffering is merely our desire to feel good?

What people fail to understand is that they are operated by something called a will to receive. The current configuration of our will to receive is what results in our lack of fulfillment in all aspects of our lives. This is precisely why most of us come to a point where we begin to feel like we are missing out on something in life. Which is why we find ourselves asking, is that all there is my friend? Wasn't there supposed to be more to life?

Since we are wired by a desire for pleasure, we are eternally slaves to the way we feel. This is the reason we do not have control of our lives, and are really not all that different from animals, except for our capacity to reason. Our reason, unfortunately, is used exclusively to weigh this dilemma of pleasure and pain. And the truth of the matter is that we cannot be fulfilled by life when we are operated by our will to receive. Every action we make is solely for us to feel good, whether it be making a charitable donation, or murdering someone for the thrill of it.

Conversely, every time we experience pleasure, our desire for pleasure grows and it becomes harder to fulfill. If you travel First Class to Cabo, you're not going to be as excited about flying Coach to Phoenix. It's our wiring. Some people will just give up, realizing the work is not worth it, while others will exhaust themselves with work to try and feel the same pleasure, but really lack for a private plane.

We're all like drug addicts looking for the pleasure of that first hit, in every single facet of our lives. There is a constant negotiation of pleasure and pain in our senses and we always choose the maximum pleasure with the minimal amount of effort. We strive for comfort constantly. Even the act of adjusting the way we sit down is really a desire for a more pleasurable state. The consequences of our actions become less and less important when we are driven by our desire for pleasure. Even if we are unaware of the harm we are doing to others, we are harming people with our innate selfishness.

A friend of mine told me a story that illustrates our nature and the nature of the society we live in. He offered, "I have a wealthy landlord who chooses to raise the rent year. I need to ask my mother for help, who also doesn't have the money. She is suffering to help me. He doesn't have any bad intentions other than profit. However, because he wants to receive money, he is harming me and countless others." This creates a cycle of harming individuals in the search for profit in both a literal and metaphorical sense.

There is however a solution to our lack of fulfillment. If we could nourish ourselves with different values, it would be impossible for us to feel a lack of purpose. We need to fulfill the other person's desire to the same extent as our own. This will allow us to achieve a different kind of fulfillment. If we were to make an unnatural effort to think of others before our self, we could temper the never-ending cycle of suffering. When we think about other people, we see that everything we felt we were missing is now fulfilled inside of us. This is the means of building an environment based on connection and mutually beneficial values. If society were to begin to think this way, we would be free of the slavery of thinking only of ourselves and achieve a new sense of freedom.

ACHIEVING EQUIVALENCE

After years of being brought in and out of a loathsome state, with little hints of unimaginable bliss scattered along the way, the Creator brings man into the attainment of *Elohim*. I use the word *Elohim*, as Creator (*Bore*) never meant anything to me. I feel God or *Hashem* (one without name) has more weight, but it's not quite accurate. *Elohim* more accurately translates to the Creating God than the Creator, or God the Creator. The Hebrew word for Elohim—in gematria (the numerical study of Torah)—, is equal to *haTevha*, Nature. Thus, God is Nature and God is in a continual state of creating, what Kabbalah describes as a state of bestowal. This is the state where one receives from *Elohim* in order to share his reception of light with the world.

Humanity has come into a state of development in direct opposition to bestowal. As the Torah knew over 3000 years ago, man's nature is evil. Entirely evil, as man is always striving to benefit himself above anything else. In opposition with Nature, man's nature is to receive pleasure at the expense of others. Nature, though it is perpetually changing and not perfect in a measurable way the way ecologists once assumed, it too is in its own state of perfection. It is in the exactly correct form for one to overcome his nature to find *Elohim's* nature. You do this through years of overcoming your desires in an *Assyria*, a sort of minion of ten friends who follow the guidelines of Kabbalah. These ten friends become a microcosm of a Kabbalah group, whose achievements influence the other *Assyria's*.

Though Nature may take a seemingly chaotic form that cybernetics, climatology and ecology have failed to classify, let alone predict, it achieves its own balance. This is why we see ill effects of African animals like hippos taking reign of one of Pablo Escobar's abandoned estates. This is why bugs become resistance to pesticides, antibiotics lose their efficacy when abused and the raping of the trees of rain forest is causing global warming instead of expanding the research of the medicinal properties of all the plants the place has been bestowed with. Rather than innovate within our means, we destroy with our desire for more. Governments, people, businesses and the markets themselves are operated on the assumption that people will choose greed at all costs. It's kind of the *Wall Street* "greed is good mantra," mixed with absolutist understanding of Ayn Rand and game theory.

The computer models are unprepared for things that have never happened before, making accounting for the majority impossible as the future itself is unpredictable. Another problem with these models is that man does not act entirely in an easily measurable self-interest, it exists entirely in the will to receive pleasure, which manifests in men choosing the most pleasure with the least effort. These choices are not simple to measure.

For many this results in people doing things that seem altruistic, to garner respect or a natural desire. Only psychopaths exclusively receive pleasure from hurting others, but receiving pleasure at the expense of others is an attribute of humanity. Only highly developed people in corporeality often called CEOs, narcissists and sociopaths actually follow the model of self-interested game theory, but they are largely responsible for the systems that determine corporeal existence and live under the assumption that everyone else works in this manner.

There is another small group that works in pure self-interest. It is those approaching a spiritual degree. They actually see the world in such a black and white manner as the result of their desire to reform their selfish nature. Their goodness opens up pleasure in the ego. Only when this desire for altruistic pleasure becomes intolerable pain, can they find the point of connection with the Creator to attain spirituality.

This is also why Nature cannot be measured or predicted. Much like nature, the form of bestowal is imperceptible to those who still exist in man's evil inclination. However, spirituality can be measured as it exists in an entirely black and white form. All that exists in spirituality is darkness and light.

One can only come to spiritual attainment by being willing to die for it. This is because when one is able to overcome his nature, by coming to equivalence of form with Nature, he perceives the world in an opposite form. What once felt good in the will to receive will feel bitter in the will to bestow. What once felt like a burden, benefitting others above the self, will feel blissful. While people perceive weakness and humility as spiritual attributes, some situations call for the exact opposite. Since *Elohim* is strong and powerful, those who attain him must be as well.

PURIM: DRUNKEN COSTUME PARTY, OR AN OPPORTUNITY TO CORRECT THE WORLD, OR BOTH?

The holiday of Purim is relevant to the Jewish people today, because it illustrates how to combat the spiritual law that is both the cause of anti-Semitism and all the suffering in the world. While most people think of Purim as a celebration, chockfull of hamantaschen, drinking and costumes, the reason behind the celebration is often lost. Furthermore, the inner meaning of the narrative of Esther and Mordechai is hidden from traditional Jewish scripture. If the deeper meaning of the story were apparent to the Jews of the world, we would see Purim's importance and use the story as a model for our world.

In its simplest terms, Purim celebrates Mordechai's defiance of King Achashverosh's advisor Haman and the salvation of the Jewish people in Achashverosh's vast empire by Mordechai's niece, the beautiful Queen Esther. The irony of the story is that although Achashverosh was about to annihilate the Jewish people, his most beloved wife was Jewish, though she concealed this from him.

When Mordecai became aware of Haman's plan to rid the nation of the insolent Jews who looked to a greater God than the King, he begged his niece Esther who he had raised like a daughter to fight for the survival of the Jewish people, by pleading for mercy from the King. This was by no means any easy task. According to the law of the time, to meet with a King unannounced was punishable by death. This situation begs one to ask a lot of questions. If this was the case, why was Esther spared and why did Achashverosh help the Jews and even hang Haman where Mordechai was supposed to be hanged? And more relevant to our time, if anti-Semitism is a fixed law, what did Mordechai and Esther do to make Achashverosh sympathize with the Jewish people? Wouldn't he see the Jews as a pest to his empire?

Like it is written in the Megillah, Haman, a trusted royal advisor, said to his King Achashverosh, there is one nation that is scattered around all the other nations, 127 nations, and because they are scattered we have an opportunity to kill them, to destroy them, to completely annihilate them. The nation he spoke of was the Jewish people and like Adolph Hitler, it seemed perfectly logical to Haman to rid the world of those who had a higher calling than the authority of their ruler. Because he felt their lack of unity, he hated them. Under the threat of imminent death, Mordechai and his ten sons were able to get all the Jews in Persia to fast and pray for three days together. Since they knew the system of the ten klipot, they were able to access the force of bestowal by unifying the Jewish people.

When Mordechai convinced Esther to speak to her husband, King Achashverosh, she was armed with the power of the unity that was transferred by the great Kabbalist Mordechai to her. In Kabbalistic terms, Mordechai was the force of connection that was able to access the force of Malchut (Esther). Endowed with this force,

Esther was able to connect with the upper force of Zeir Anpin (The Creator and Achashverosh). In short, the force of unity was what protected her and saved the Jewish people. The King Achashverosh, the symbol of the Creator in the story, only protected the Jews because they were united with the force of Malchut. This expresses that when the Jewish people are united they are not only spared affliction from the Creation, but are loved by all the nations of the world.

The Jewish people are in just as critical a time in their history as Mordechai and Esther, but they do not recognize this is the case, because they don't have a clear Haman or a Hitler to spark a desire to unite. One sees very clearly without an immediate threat to their security the Jewish people don't have any motivation to unite. Only when they are under attack do the Jewish people have such a necessity. In Israel, last year it was very clear that when rockets were fired, the Jewish people felt a need to unite, just as the foundation of Israel was only possible after the atrocities of the Holocaust. However, we see very little effort to unite when the signs of anti-Semitism appear minor, unrelated and scattered across the world. Essentially people stay inert unless they feel an immediate threat to their security and even when that threat came, their egos held onto the belief their status and possessions could protect them. More troubling, when one looks to history, it is clear that without a direct threat to their right to exist, Jews let anti-Semitism happen until it is too late to minimize the damage.

What the Jewish people need to understand is that they are special. They were endowed with a point in the heart that gives them an opportunity to restore order in an increasingly tortured world. In their DNA exists the capacity to unite, but nothing will change until they awaken the Creator with their unity. If the Jewish people wait for the next Haman, they are working in "due time," meaning that further atrocities like those that were experienced seventy years ago are inevitable. By connecting like Mordechai, Jews have the opportunity to "hasten the times," to prevent unnecessary tragedy. In such a state, Jews will internally rise above their egoistic desires and create the framework for a better world, a place where no nations need borders and people will intuitively know how to care for each other above their own needs and evil desires.

Purim is the time of the year where the Jewish people have the possibility to create such a world. Though not celebrated with the same fervor as some of the other holidays, it is written that Purim is the one holiday that will remain in a corrected world. This is because it is the one holiday that clearly explains how to attain the goal of correction. On Purim, Jews around the world get drunk. Though they may not be aware of it, Jews drink so they do not differentiate between the force of Haman—the ego—and the force of Mordechai, the small force of bestowal that is connected to the Upper Force of Creation. When Jews drink on Purim, they are able to work above their reason—when you're drunk you lose the capacity to think—and see that there is no difference between good and evil. By recognizing this, it becomes clear to the Jewish people that only through connection can Jews work for the sake of bestowal and the correction of the entire world. If the Jews of the world want to unite and rid the world of all its problems including anti-Semitism, Purim is the time. The great Kabbalist, the Rabash, foretold that once the world is corrected, Purim will be the only holiday we celebrate.

Designed by Josia Nakash

I'M STUDYING TORAH: HOW THE EGOISTIC WORLD WILL PRODUCE ANGELS

"I place upon them a king such as Haman, and he will force them to repent."

The world is approaching a state of complete darkness. Only through these conditions can the light awaken.

We should strive for divine will, the final correction that illuminates not only the state of the world, but gives us the means to piece together what ails us. The great Kabbalist, Baruch Ashlag (The Rabash) writes, "The order of the work in Torah and *Mitzvot* begins with *Lo Lishma* [not for Her name; for one's own benefit], as it is written in *The Zohar*, "Some keep Torah and *Mitzvot* in order to be rewarded in this world, and some work in Torah and *Mitzvot* to have the next world." However, his reward is only what he will receive in his vessels of self-reception, which is considered earthliness. This manner is called "people of the earth," meaning that they do not move from the earth, which is called the "will to receive.""

The world was moving forward through the ego and after the time of the Rashi (11th century), egoistic development in the Jews was in line and in fact greater than those building empires at the expense of common people. They were however united and devoted to God, devoid of fantasy, clung to their Creator and aware he didn't exist without their mutual love and exertion. Though many acquired vast wealth, they lived in simplicity, hated idols and lived separately from the Egyptians (not the people but the egoistic and material aims of man).

Now no one lives in service of the Creator. The religious work became exclusively for one's own egoistic development. This creates a problem within the religious who see themselves as righteous, when they are actually more egoistic than the majority.

No one wants to hear how empty they are, because their intention is incorrect. The klipot (shells that block light and connection with the Creator) of religion has corrupted spiritual matters throughout history and now there is no positive element in traditional *lo lishma* (for personal benefit) religious devotion. People believe by performing actions they are pleasing the Creator regardless of their intention, when they are damaging the world more than the secular.

Though throughout history many people in attainment were largely the result of their dedication to the nature of the *mitzvot* (following laws and customs, praying), they worked against their desire. We see today that the younger generations, especially those most developed mostly believe in nothing. This nothingness is actually the right tool for our development into a world of sanctity. Though we no longer are driven by shame and honor, our desires have developed to a point wherein all our lusts are easily fulfilled.

There is limitless reception of everything one could ever want and at a fair price or for free. The internet is mostly free or easy to steal from. Though it seems the nihilism this produces is a vulgarity that puts Satan over our shoulder it does the exact opposite. The world will soon see that the Creator is aiding us through these corruptions.

It is easy to open up the desires when we learn that nothing is real and that we will never be fulfilled. This is happening on a huge scale in the egoistic world before us. It means we want something more. Sex has even begun to lose some of its flavor and that's good, because the failure of sex for one's own pleasure will lead one to the infinite pleasure of bestowing in order to receive. We will build a world of love without religions, without borders that fights the battle of *lishma* (for the sake of the Creator) to receive what the Creator bestows upon us with open arms, casting aside the evil inclination for one's self and we will see clearly that this inclination only drives us to become faithful soldiers to the Creator! We will live as angels without limits, as pure divine rods of love. Angels have free will, but evil is not an option for them.

REPAIRING THE SHATTERED WORLD IN FOUR PHASES

All of reality exists in the single thought of Creation. It is unbound by time and ever-flowing. Kabbalists want to access the unchanging, infinite energy that exists in this thought of the Upper system of Creation. Attaining spirituality is the ability to develop a sense of the Upper World, the thought of Creation manifested as the light of the Creator. This goal depends on a properly formed group of people aimed towards unity, oneness and love.

Israel was once in a perfect state of light and connection. The desire for oneness will restore this when humans learn to live in the light of the Creator. Anyone with the right desire has the opportunity to realize this goal, in the same breadth and measure as Adam, Moses and King David.

This seems unreachable in today's world, which is so distant from divinity. In our desire, everything we do is for our own benefit, because we live in complete darkness. When we achieve spirituality, we awaken the light and our perception is shaped by our ability to "love thy friend as thyself."

Achieving this perception of the world as a single system of love and connection is done in four stages. Though one can understand this process, these stages are complicated by the limitations of humankind's perception. This corruption of thought and desire, is why few people attain spirituality in the world today.

For Adam, this process was relatively easy, as he had a pure and simple desire. He was not corrupted by the egoistic development that exists in the world today that distances us from the light of God. In our advancement, it will feel like we are moving backwards and forwards all at once.

There are number of reasons for this, but the main obstacle is that as human beings without vessels of bestowal (a desire to give to others without self-concern) a person can't perceive bestowal. We don't even know what bestowal is. Whenever we strive to build this desire, our bodies fight us, because our default setting is to receive pleasure only for own benefit.

Adding to the confusion, time is not linear in spirituality. This is the result of all the phases being a single interconnected process. All four phases are dependent on each other, develop gradually and are included in each discernment of the four phases. Everything one experiences in his or her spiritual growth is dependent on how one is tuned that system. This includes all the discernments and levels of attainment, which are processed through the entire system of all five worlds. These worlds constitute the totality of reality, which is only light and darkness that a person in spirituality receives through filters.

This is the system where the Creator's light flows through man above time and space, connecting man to the reality of God. While many have faith in a Creator, only by accessing the vessels of bestowal and becoming part of the system can one know Him.

This system is only built by a person's connection with a Kabbalah group, through connection to the original sources and the hearts of others. One cannot overcome his or her own nature by one's own forces, so a person depends on a group to hold him. More precisely, one becomes dependent on a microcosm of his or her group, "the ten." A ten is a minion of ten Kabbalists that function as a single body to build the ten parts of each world from *malchut* (mouth, reception) to *keter* (crown, bestowing light, wisdom) and back to *malchut* in an elliptical process.

When one first receives the light, it's a small opening derived from a spark. One has a point in the heart that compels him or her to want to understand the meaning of the world. This person senses a force is operating them and they want to know that unchanging force of the Creator. He is only infinite light of pure goodness. A person progressively receives greater portions of the light by becoming more and more like the Creator. While by and large the Kabbalists were Jewish, the soul of Creation extends to everyone regardless of race, religion or nationality.

If a person has this desire they are part of the shattering, the broken vessel of the system of Adam HaRishon, one of the 600,000 disconnected pieces born 5700 years ago when Eve ate from the tree of knowledge. While this is the image the Torah provides, she didn't actually bite from the apple of the serpent. Adam's desire for knowledge is the meaning of the above-mentioned parable. He was the first person whose knowledge allowed him to split the spiritual from the corporeal. So, though he sinned with his desire for knowledge, he also created the Creator with his curiosity. Before him, life was only animalistic pleasure without free will.

There have been a few times when the shattering Adam instigated was corrected. If you have a point in the heart, your soul has a memory (*reshimot*) of when Israel was connected as one, as it was in

Abraham's tent, at Moses' reception of the Torah at Mount Sinai and during the first and second temples of Jerusalem. In all these corporeal forms, the light of the Creator was in tune the people.

Each phase of direct light orients us closer to this state, where we can feel the Creator's unchanging, infinite force in more flavor and precision. This infinite force cannot be described in words, but we call it *Atzmutot* (His essence). The Creator is always giving us infinite light, but we are not connected with it. It's like we're receiving empty white noise from a radio and need to adjust to the right station. Together in a single intention we can turn the dial and restore Israel to a state of sanctity. This adjustment happens in four phases of direct light.

The first stage in this process is *Behina Aleph*, which means first phase. This is the first level of reception from the broken vessel of Adam HaRishon. The vessel receives knowledge (*hochma*) of bestowal. This is the previously described awakening of the point in the heart, the first discernment that man makes in his will to receive for one's self. One's reason tells a person that it is better to give to others than to receive for one's own benefit.

In the second phase (*Behina Bet*), like Adam HaRishon, one crosses the *machsom*, the barrier between corporeality and spirituality. One has knowledge that it is better to bestow than to receive, but the body only has a desire for self-reception. This results in the body rejecting the light of the Creator. This rejection is the source of the conception of the *sephira* (one of ten *sephirot*, attributes of the Creator contained in each world) *bina* (goodness, strength). This is working above one's nature to the build the quality of bestowal. The quality of bestowal is built in the man by emptying his or her vessel, creating a state of complete darkness in the vessel for the light to enter.

The third phase (*Behina Gimel*) is where one builds *Zeir Anpin* (small face), the partially revealed aspect of the Creator. This is where one has awareness of the Creator operating him in his senses, as he or she is illuminated with the light of *Hassadim* (mercy). Light of *Hassadim* sorts out the contradiction of the light of *bina* and the light of *hochma*, and better orients a person to receive the light, so he or she will eventually be able to bestow it to others through his connection to those with the same desire.

The Creator's mercy brings the created being perception of the thought of Creation, turning one's self into a creature by rising above the aforementioned mixed discernments and receiving a small portion of the Creator's light (20%) in the first world of Assiya. This degree of light is illuminated on the first world always, but the receiver perceives it differently depending on the differences in *klipot* (shells that block the Creator's light), concealments of faith, and *masachim* (screens, blockages in the purity of the soul).

The reception of the light of *Hassadim* brings about the final phase of direct light (*Behina Dalet*). This is the degree of *malchut* (mouth, reception, king). *Malchut* is the female desire of reception, the desire to become like the Creator, to receive the light of the Creator in order to bestow contentment to him by bestowing to his creatures. The creature achieves independence from the Creator by achieving equivalence of form with him, but his or her desire is only for the Creator to feel joy and rid him of the suffering the uncorrected creatures cause him.

When a group of many Assyria's work for this desire, the result is the foundation of a vessel. This vessel is built to be oriented to the will of the Creator, both for the Assyria and the individual, which become one. A mutual deficiency (*hissaron*) gives the group the power to inherit the Torah. The Assyria's and the group itself receives from Him, the ability to receive in order to bestow. The group becomes like the arms and legs of the Creator. This is why the great Kabbalist Baal HaSulam writes, "The Torah (light), the Creator and Israel (the Kabbalah group) are one."

(by Meirav Rasumni)

THE END OF RATIONALITY

Reason is entirely subjective.

When the great Kabbalist Baal HaSulam, made the decision to look at Kabbalah from a purely scientific lens, he was living in a rational age. There was a fundamental belief that everything could be understood scientifically. The Soviet Union was a perceived threat to the global order, as they were determined to use analytical models to build a perfect rational society according to the philosophy of Karl Marx. Trotsky held a religious belief that rational models would heighten the mind and productivity of individuals until "the average person would be an Aristotle, a Goethe, a Marx." This utopian system did work for a time (of course not to the extent of Trotsky's vision), especially under the iron fist of Stalin making the models work by killing all detractors.

Today we are aware that looking at the world from a rational perspective is irrational. Life is racked with contradictions and though governments and economies still adhere to computer models, these models fail to account for unforeseen cataclysms (natural disasters, 9/11, 2008 financial crisis) that are inevitable. On a more fundamental level they fail to account for the irrational nature of humanity. Nevertheless, the inherently flawed belief that things can be easily categorized by computer calculations is widespread by those in charge, the so-called experts who sit twiddling their thumbs every few years when "the unthinkable" happens.

Last year two historic events clearly articulated the flaw of analytical data and the inability of experts to properly assess them. These of course were Brexit and the election of Trump. The two events, though statistically probable were seen as unthinkable by anyone with a voice in the media or anyone with real power on the corporeal plane of existence.

No one is rational. This is why experts were flabbergasted when these two somewhat likely occurrences occurred. The main reasons these events happened was because people are inherently irrational creatures that have lost faith in the institutions that once held things together.

Today, the order of society is broken. People are aware they are being lied to by those who purport to be objective. Most people don't really care, until a flaw in the thinking of the objective thinkers takes their job away. When things are normal, they sit in front of Facebook and the limitless selection of watchable television suited to every subculture of humanity. When people are hurt by the breaking of the system, they have irrational emotional reactions.

There is an inherent distrust of the rational, because the results of rational thinking have only damaged the world. Communism, socialism and even pure capitalism no longer work for the majority. This utter disconnection and distrust is the opportunity for the spiritual to blend with the corporeal. The opening for a revolution in the consciousness of humanity.

The system of creation is a spiritual realm outside the sensations of everyone with the exception of a small collection of souls connected by the light of God. Kabbalah works by fixed rules. It is scientific, but not provable with the means of the scientific method in our current age of development. Only those who attain the upper force have a means of quantifying the machinations of the spiritual world. Like everything else in life it is full of many contradictions that people of a rational bent (the educated classes) can't quite grasp (though it was an obsession of 20th century scientists and philosophers such as Carl Jung, Walter Benjamin and Sigmund Freud). It is a system of perfect opposite forces, good and evil or light and darkness. When evil is revealed, the desire for good forces one of a spiritual nature to do good and connect directly with the Creator.

Those few people connected to the opposite forces are called Kabbalists. They are connected to a rational system of light that manifests in a way that those with corporeal senses cannot comprehend. This is even true of many who devote their lives entirely to the wisdom. This is because the light of God is working directly through the Kabbalists and it is perfect. In any given moment, it accounts for all the details of creation that are changing at a pace that no computer could measure. This is because God, I prefer Elohim (the creating force) is unlimited by the limited minds of humans who program the computers. This will be true even when these computers acquire artificial intelligence.

The Creator is an unchanging force without an image that is immeasurably smarter than humanity. Unlike man and everything man purports to be objective, God is objective. Like a sage of Kabbalah, He accounts for the ever-changing system of nature in its totality. Both the spiritual and the corporeal that are inextricably linked to one another.

THE ABSENCE OF SHAME, SOCIAL INJUSTICE, AUTOMATION, WELFARE AND REDEMPTION

Culture is dissolving because lies are presented as inarguable truth, especially to the educated classes and the majority of the young elites (i.e. Silicon Valley, academics). The closer one comes to wisdom the further they are from the conventions of the day. Wisdom and reason are usually opposing forces, as reason is really a means of making subjective opinion objective truth by self-interested people. As one with a curious mind grows older, one finds that the virtues blindly offered as inarguable truth have something very sinister at their roots. Some things are presented as fact, when they are anything but. These flat out lies foment disruption and disunity.

Some examples of utter bullshit passing as falsifiable truth are as follows: it is better to explore diversity of cultures than to impose positive shared values on diverse communities; all cultures hold equal values; it's pretentious and elitist to know things about history, reason, political structures, culture and religion; democracy works regardless of whether the public is informed; all political parties are equally bad; happiness comes mostly from being true to one's self; and finally, self-interest is preferable to wisdom and love.

Since man once knew their self-interest was a destructive force, people fought their selfish qualities. Self-interest was shameful. Thus, most people sought to sacrifice for the betterment of their communities and were happier with smaller desires. Even if they were shamelessly self-interested, virtually all people still made sacrifices for the people they loved. Today, the masses live absent of shame in their pursuit of acquiring more for themselves at the expense of others, while believing in their inherent goodness stemming from socially progressive values. I believe all this degradation stems from the reversal of one position. Mankind used to believe they were inherently evil, while today they believe their nature is good. They have lost the understanding that the development of culture is the only reason Cincinnati isn't composed of tribal warlords.

While some 17th and 18th century philosophers posited that man is inherently good, it was a minority opinion. Shame and fear of God no longer matter even to those who purport to hold religious and/or ideological beliefs. While religion still has a transcendent effect on what people will or will not do in their personal lives, those with "virtuous" political stances make no effort to enact these values in their relationships with others.

The most vocal leftist voices are elites who purport to be socialists, who don't pay their fair share of taxes and live walled off from society in their many vacation homes, paying a lower percent of tax on earned income than waitresses. All people basically do whatever they want as long as they can get away with it.

Religions, like most other institutions have lost their credibility, so virtue signaling has become its own kind of dogma. This is why it has become socially reprehensible for those in the Upper Middle Class to support Israel, Christianity, strong borders, law and order and a host of other things that in and of themselves are no different than the policies of the Democratic Party a decade ago.

If Martin Luther King were to make the "I have a dream" speech today it would be deemed culturally insensitive as it is in direct opposition to the calling card of multiculturalism. Rather than dream of a world above racial divisions, where black and white children live as one, Americans now are indoctrinated with a message that our differences in culture should be highlighted. American values, such as a basic understanding of civic responsibility and upward mobility are dissolving and viewed as old fashioned, snobbish and racist. Instead of celebrating the exceptionalism of the ideal that anyone can be president with a bit of luck, intelligence and work ethic, curriculums are founded on the inherent unfairness of America.

Instead of feeling shame that one does not achieve anything meaningful, or strive to make the world better, young people are taught to blame the powers that be and that by donating five dollars to intrinsically flawed charities by text message they are doing their part to make the world a better place.

Though it is a compelling argument that banks have too much power and are structured as tools of oppression, people are not limited by anything but their lack of courage and lack of connection. This is a systemic problem as the world is building an environment that teaches people to blame others and divide by shared interests and ethnicities. Young people often give up on their dreams too easily. Though they dream of a fair world of more inclusive values, they tend to distract themselves with entertainment, developing as individuals splintered into subcultures. Without a shared sense of responsibility these bloated desires eventually lose their luster and we end up with depressed people living in a nihilistic culture.

The lack of shame also bleeds into the economy and governments. When a Jew was in trouble say a hundred years ago, he would get help from his synagogue. This would cause shame in the individual, leading him to devote himself to God with more power and find the means to repay the charity he or she was given. Today, social welfare has huge swathes of the population receiving aid from the government absent of shame. The person is taking anonymously from an entity without a face with no incentive to change one's situation. Most of the time the person receiving the aid is penalized for turning their life around. As robotics become cheaper this looks to get even worse.

Automation has gradually streamlined production, so that there is an abundance of resources without a need for workers. Many are predicting that robots will replace the majority of workers, requiring and potentially paying for universal basic income. In our lifetime, we may see the majority of the people in developed countries given a decent salary for sitting at home all day. The main beneficiaries look to be junk food manufacturers and drugdealers in my humble eyes.

Inevitably a populace without a purpose in life will become more depressed and nihilistic. While what is presented above looks like a hopeless state, only from complete darkness can a revolution in consciousness occur. As the great Kabbalist Isaiah Horowitz wrote in the early 17th century, "At the end of our suffering, at the time of redemption, not only will we return to the degree of greatness that we had before, but there will be a great advantage for the future light, a great many degrees over what was before, and this exalted advantage comes about by the force of darkness and troubles." This is because redemption comes from sorrow.

Kabbalists describe a world above our current senses where all that exists is light and darkness, a sensation that lifts us above this world where pure pleasure emanates from our connection. Only in a spiritual lull is it possible to alter the broken consciousness of the world that does not yet feel the necessity for love above self-interest. Unfortunately, it requires a time where most things feel meaningless to most people. Universal basic income is bound to be that catalyst.

The free time afforded to the majority and the depression it will ultimately cause, will be an opportunity for the people to recalibrate themselves to the forces above this world. They will be forced to turn to God. Since religion has lost its authority over most, this connection with God will be for all the people in the world with a desire to answer the big question, "What is the meaning of my life?"

When a large group of people all collectively feel the hopelessness of humanity, a spark will awaken in their hearts to know God and the gates of wisdom will open before them. From a state of disconnection people will be compelled to connect above their differences and their nature to restore balance as virtually every sphere of society is on the verge of crisis. The only antidote to widespread depression and dissatisfaction is connection and unity. While it will take a lot of collective sacrifice, this sacrifice promises the formation of a better world that will work in concert with the imperceptible goodness and perfection of the Creator, who is crying out for the world to be redeemed.

The Creator will be known as people without anything but time will be drawn to the knowledge that humanity's true purpose, "is the fulfillment of the duties of the heart — to acknowledge the Unity of God in our hearts, to believe in Him, to love Him, resign our souls to Him, and make His name the unifying central thought of all our conduct," as Bahya ibn Paquda wisely advised in the 11th century. People will see that wisdom comes from simple actions that come with little recognizable reward, that fulfillment comes from devotion to God through connecting with and loving others above everything that divides us.

(Photo by Alma Gustafsson)

UNCONDITIONAL LOVE

We are naturally as humans drawn to certain people who influence our actions. Most people have about ten. We think we are guided by our own choices, but what determines our values is the guidance of who we respect most and who we are closest to. In modernity, these nine people irrespective of ourselves are in a constant state of flux.

When I examine my own life, this list changes so fast I probably couldn't accurately track it. My parents of course play a very large role in the group of ten. Some good friends who I think are cool and had things I wanted also played a large role in the ten. I could easily annul my own preferences to theirs unconsciously. Often the guiding force was a celebrity, film director, or fellow author. They could be either alive or dead. In my book, *The Egotist*, I account for how I was very proud of my development into quite an individual. While I believed that I was choosing my preferences that guided my individual development, I was a slave to what brought me pleasure. I was handcuffing myself with my ego, until it was unbearable for me and everyone around me.

Corporeal love generally lasts between one and two years. This love is more accurately described as lust. What develops in spiritual relationships is something that grows above the lust and corporeal friendship. By being pleasant to one another, these relationships often lose their luster for fear of hating one another.

When people love, it creates fear, fear of losing the love and the person. There is also the constant fear that the person on the opposite end of the telephone doesn't feel the same way, they don't hear your thoughts, or intuitively understand you the way you feel they do. This creates undue hatred and envy. In a normal relationship, this generally leads to divorce, dissolving friendships, building resentments, hating each other on the surface and passive-aggressively.

In spirituality, the hatred that develops is overcome with a higher degree of love, pure love where one learns to care about the needs of another person. Many people claim to experience this in corporeal vessels, but it is always a lie. One's ego always determines the level of the amount they perceive love. There is always self-benefit.

One can come to a spiritual state out of enslavement to the ego, by transcending one's natural preferences, by deciding to place spiritual ascendance above all other calculations. The student consciously decides to make the ten students the only environment that influences them. In a Kabbalah group with a teacher in attainment of the spiritual worlds, a student annuls himself to nine relative strangers, overtaking the nine natural determining forces in one's life. All one has to do is annul their own desire for pleasure entirely to a desire to bring the other nine students pleasure under the guidance of Kabbalistic sources. One chooses to want to lift the friend above this world, more than he or she wants it for one's self. He or she becomes part of the other nine, loving the friend unconditionally.

The work we do as messengers of the Creator is simple. We connect and annul above our reason. The only obstacle is our ego that grows as a direct inverse of the sacrifice we make. This is why one must decide to make a *brit* (a covenant). The problem with the *brit* as it stands now for most who try and annul is the development of the ego inverse relation to their desire to help the friend. It becomes nearly impossible to care for the other friend, as their ego makes them care only for one's self.

Under such conditions, one is not being honest with one's self, since they're adhering to the will of the group and doing actions absent of intention. The intention is to overcome one's desire, but man must know what his desire is, what holds importance over the Creator, why they are unable to see the Creator as the only authority. If one does not examine and account for these things honestly, their prayers for the collective are not heard Above.

After one does the work absent of intention, they create an empty space. One sees the impossibility of caring for someone else as much as they care about their own comfort and security. They are filled with darkness and despair, but this despair without any hope of exit allows one to lift above this world and become part of the force of the Creator. They can love others unconditionally out of a natural inclination forever.

ABOUT THE AUTHOR

Jesse Bogner is an author, screenwriter and journalist. His memoir and social critique, *The Egotist*, has been translated into four languages. In 2013, he moved from New York City, where he was born and for the most part raised, abandoning a decadent lifestyle chockfull of substance abuse, to study Kabbalah in Israel. His work has been featured in The Daily Caller, The Huffington Post, The Jerusalem Post and The Times of Israel. He has been featured in misleading articles from media outlets including CNN, Wired Magazine and others. He is currently writing a novel.

CONTACT

Burning Bush
Publishing

jesse@jessebogner.com

Jesse Bogner
1816 Glenwood Rd.
Brooklyn, NY 11230